P9-CES-126

DOVER · THRIFT · EDITIONS

The Cavalier Poets

AN ANTHOLOGY

EDITED BY
THOMAS CROFTS

DOVER PUBLICATIONS, INC.
New York

DOVER THRIFT EDITIONS

GENERAL EDITOR: STANLEY APPELBAUM
EDITOR OF THIS VOLUME: THOMAS CROFTS

Contents

Copyright

Published in Canada by General Publishing Company, Ltd., 30 Lesmill Road, Don Mills, Toronto, Ontario.

Published in the United Kingdom by Constable and Company, Ltd., 3 The Lanchesters, 162–164 Fulham Palace Road, London W6 9ER.

Bibliographical Note

The Cavalier Poets: An Anthology is a new selection of works by Robert Herrick (from *Hesperides* and *Noble Numbers*, both 1648), Thomas Carew (from *Poems*, 1651), Sir John Suckling (from *Fragmenta Aurea*, 1648, and *Last Remains*, 1659) and Richard Lovelace (from *Lucasta*, 1659), reprinted from standard editions, first published by Dover Publications, Inc., in 1995. The introductory Note, introductions to each of the poets and the Index of first lines have been specially prepared for this edition.

Library of Congress Cataloging-in-Publication Data

The Cavalier poets : an anthology / edited by Thomas Crofts.
     p.   cm. — (Dover thrift editions)
  ISBN 0-486-28766-1 (pbk.)
  1. English poetry—Early modern, 1500–1700. 2. Royalists—Great Britain. I. Crofts, Thomas, 1968–   . II. Series.
  PR1209.C25 1995
  821'.408—dc20
                                                95-23527
                                               CIP

Manufactured in the United States of America
Dover Publications, Inc., 31 East 2nd Street, Mineola, N.Y. 11501

Note

The reign of Charles I (1625–1649) is remembered as one of England's most turbulent periods. Through the House of Commons, the nation was voicing a general discontent with the policies of the King, and in general questioning the traditional absolute power of the monarchy. Charles, though he had many good qualities, was utterly unsuited to the challenge these issues presented to the royal office. His tragic flaw lay precisely in his idea of the monarchy's supreme privilege and unquestionable power. A king, he thought, should rule absolutely, judge according to his own wisdom and elevate the kingdom by his benevolence and personal magnificence. In this scheme not much emphasis was put upon economics or political ethics.

Charles, of course, failed miserably with Parliament, which asked him to compromise his absolute hegemony on issues 'of taxation and religion, among the era's thorniest topics. In the absence of cooperation between King and Parliament, taxes were levied almost arbitrarily with no attempt at fairness. Also, the rising influence of the Puritans, combined with the rebellious and highly aggravated Presbyterian Scots—against whom Charles waged the Bishops' Wars of 1639 and 1640—urged reform of the kingdom's strict laws regarding worship. But Charles only convened Parliament in order to ask for money, and when money was refused him, he dissolved the Parliament (he did this many times, in fact ruling for eleven years of his reign without convening Parliament once).

This arrogance alienated him from most of his kingdom, causing him to rely, as his father James I had done (somewhat more successfully), on court advisers such as George Villiers, Duke of Buckingham; William Laud, Bishop of London; and Thomas Wentworth, Earl of Strafford. In the meantime, Charles waged unpopular and costly wars (against Spain and Scotland) and made questionable arrangments for cash (including forced loans from the gentry).

The open hostility between King and Parliament having grown for seventeen years unchecked by conciliatory efforts from either side, the English Civil War effactually began well before actual fighting broke out in 1642. In early June of that year, Parliament made a final appeal to Charles, submitting to him the *Nineteen Propositions*, which addressed pressing issues, notably among them church reform and methods of Parliamentary appointment. Charles rejected them. Shortly thereafter sides were drawn between the "Roundheads" (Parliamentarians, Puritans) and the "Cavaliers"

(Royalists, Episcopalians) and skirmishes began. In all, Charles's forces managed a noble fight, scoring several unlikely victories, but were finally no match for the Roundhead forces led by Oliver Cromwell. The Cavaliers were defeated decisively at the Battle of Naseby (June 14, 1645). Negotiations with the King were attempted, but Charles's continued obstinacy led to his arrest at Oxford in 1647. At the last, Charles was deposed, kept captive and finally executed (beheaded January 30, 1649).

If this was one of England's most turbulent moments politically, it was also one of its richest literary periods. As in the political arena, poets of the age can be divided into two distinct "schools" (though coexisting peacefully). The two poetic leaders of this age were Ben Jonson and John Donne. Followers of Donne, the "Metaphysicals" included George Herbert, Henry Vaughan, Thomas Traherne and Richard Crashaw, who, like their master, tried in their introspective, meditative poetry to cultivate a parallel universe of metaphor, using intensely artificial, complex and sometimes grotesque imagery in the exploration of (mostly) spiritual subjects. The followers of Ben Jonson, on the other hand (who, in fact called themselves "The Tribe of Ben" or "The Sons of Ben"), wrote a much more direct, earthy, social poetry. Jonson was the ideal Cavalier poet: he wrote of erotic love, wine and well-stocked pantries in country houses, and could also write highly personal poems about his own life, embracing both its trivialities and its tragedies. His followers, too, were devoted to the pleasures of civilization, which for them meant a benevolent, adored monarch, flourishing arts and a peaceful, unmolested populace. Despite the troubled times the Cavaliers were always supportive of Charles, but it is certain that the poets saw what was coming and in their writing one can find — what is not quite there in the writing of Jonson (who died in 1637) — an awareness of political doom and, however obliquely expressed, a feeling of dispossession. It was therefore a great era for *carpe diem* poetry (cf. Herrick's classic "To the Virgins, to Make Much of Time"). Their obvious joy in language (one of the Cavalier poets' most engaging qualities) was mixed with foreboding: the pageantry of the court was going out, and the Protectorate, Cromwell's dictatorial reign, was coming in.

NOTE: In keeping with the Dover Thrift series, spellings have been for the most part modernized, and many seventeenth-century typographical conventions (such as frequent capitalization and/or italicization of nouns) have been abandoned, though certain proper nouns, such as Villiers and Carlisle, retain their old spellings Villers and Carlile.

ROBERT HERRICK

ROBERT HERRICK (1591–1674) was the eldest and perhaps the most pious of the "Sons of Ben." Among other things, he is the master of the blithe lyric, bringing equal skill and *joie de vivre* to amorous songs, satiric couplets, pagan drinking rounds and devotional poetry (Herrick was ordained an Episcopal minister on April 24, 1623). His witty, breezy style has often been likened to that of the Roman poet Catullus. Compared to such contemporaries as John Donne and George Herbert, Herrick seems light and tripping, going out of his way to demonstrate no very complex philosophical thought or religious passion (though his devotional verses are suitably austere), and never writing a love poem that speaks profoundly or intimately of the beloved. An elegy for his father ("To the Reverend Shade of His Religious Father," page 5) is overshadowed in both length and intensity of feeling by the sack poems ("His Farewell to Sack," page 7; and "The Welcome to Sack," page 11). And both seem bested by the gusts of lusty good humor in his brief, beautiful amorous poems. This is not to say, however, that Herrick was incapable of writing with feeling. There is an accumulated emotional weight in the many Julia poems that at times is resolved in lines of great tenderness. The devotional poem "A Thanksgiving to God, for His House" has the poet, who never claims saintliness, renouncing wealth and fame (somewhat hesitatingly) for the life of a country parson. With a proudly restrained melancholy and a somewhat mournful pace, but also with tenderness, the poet describes the parts of his house and vicarage farm, the animals, the garden vegetables and the other rural things that constitute his wages.

Herrick is also the standard-bearer of the life-style of the court in the last years of Charles I. His somewhat overblown panegyrics of the well-meaning but fatally incompetent king, and his praises of Charles's military successes (which were comparatively few), now strike us as poignant.

In the period between Jonson and Dryden, Herrick is among the most important English lyric poets. By obstinately writing his brisk lyrics even during the bloody and finally cataclysmic civil war, Herrick preserved the intricacy, wit and wordplay of English Renaissance poetry. As well, he fostered a healthy atmosphere for good verse during this period, setting the example for many poets, not least the three following him in the present anthology.

On his ordination, Herrick was given the priory of Dean in Devonshire in the west of England. Here he lived, wrote and performed his holy offices busily and for the most part happily, never completely ceasing, however, to long for the citified pleasures of his native London. In 1647 he was expelled from the priory by the provisional government of the Protectorate for his outspoken support of Charles. With the ascendancy of Charles II in 1660 he was returned to the sleepy vicarage in Devon, where he died and was buried in 1674.

Note: in the following text, numbered footnotes are those of the present editor; starred and daggered footnotes are Herrick's own.

The Argument of His Book[1]

I sing of brooks, of blossoms, birds, and bowers:
Of April, May, of June, and July-flowers.
I sing of may-poles, hock-carts, wassails, wakes,
Of bride-grooms, brides, and of their bridal-cakes.
I write of youth, of love, and have access
By these, to sing of cleanly-wantonness.
I sing of dews, of rains, and piece by piece
Of balm, of oil, of spice, and amber-greece.[2]
I sing of times trans-shifting; and I write
How roses first came red, and lillies white.
I write of groves, of twilights, and I sing
The Court of Mab, and of the Fairy-King.
I write of Hell; I sing (and ever shall)
Of Heaven, and hope to have it after all.

When He Would Have His Verses Read

In sober mornings, do not thou rehearse
The holy incantation of a verse;
But when that men have both well drunk, and fed,
Let my enchantments then be sung, or read.
When laurel spirts i' th' fire, and when the hearth
Smiles to itself, and gilds the roof with mirth;
When up the Thyrse* is rais'd, and when the sound
Of sacred Orgies† flies, a round, a round.
When the rose reigns and locks with ointments shine,
Let rigid Cato read these lines of mine.[3]

---

[1]*Hesperides* (1648).
[2]*amber-greece*: ambergris.
*A Javelin twined with Ivy.
†Songs to Bacchus.
[3]*rigid Cato*: Cato the Censor (234–149 B.C.) of Rome, a man of severe morals and
   vigorous patriotism.

Upon the Loss of His Mistresses

I have lost, and lately, these
Many dainty mistresses:
Stately Julia, prime of all;
Sappho next, a principal;
Smooth Anthea, for a skin
White, and heaven-like crystalline;
Sweet Electra, and the choice
Myrrha, for the lute and voice;
Next, Corinna, for her wit,
And the graceful use of it,
With Perilla. All are gone;
Only Herrick's left alone,
For to number sorrow by
Their departures hence, and die.

The Vine

I dream'd this mortal part of mine
Was metamorphos'd to a vine;
Which crawling one and every way,
Enthrall'd my dainty Lucia.
Me thought, her long small legs & thighs
I with my tendrils did surprise;
Her belly, buttocks, and her waist,
By my soft nerv'lets were embrac'd:[1]
About her head I writhing hung,
And with rich clusters (hid among
The leaves) her temples I behung:
So that my Lucia seem'd to me
Young Bacchus ravish'd by his tree.
My curls about her neck did crawl,
And arms and hands they did enthrall:
So that she could not freely stir,
(All parts there made one prisoner).
But when I crept with leaves to hide
Those parts, which maids keep unespied,

---

[1] *nerv'lets*: tendrils.

Such fleeting pleasures there I took,
That with the fancy I awook;
And found (Ah me!) this flesh of mine
More like a stock, than like a vine.

His Request to Julia

Julia, if I chance to die
Ere I print my poetry;
I most humbly thee desire
To commit it to the fire:
Better 'twere my book were dead,
Than to live not perfected.

To the King

Upon His Coming with His Army into the West[1]

Welcome, most welcome to our vows and us,
Most great, and universal Genius![2]
The drooping West, which hitherto has stood
As one, in long-lamented-widowhood;
Looks like a bride now, or a bed of flowers,
Newly refresh'd, both by the sun, and showers.
War, which before was horrid, now appears
Lovely in you, brave Prince of Cavaliers!
A deal of courage in each bosom springs
By your access; (O you the best of Kings!)
Ride on with all white omens; so, that where
Your standard's up, we fix a conquest there.

---

[1] *into the West*: en route to Cornwall, where Charles I and the Royal army defeated
the Parliamentary militia in September of 1644. Charles would have passed
through Devon, where Herrick had his vicarage.
[2] *genius*: in the Roman sense of a local guardian deity.

To the Reverend Shade of His Religious Father

That for seven lusters[1] I did never come
To do the rites to thy religious tomb:
That neither hair was cut, or true tears shed
By me, o'er thee, (as justments to the dead)
Forgive, forgive me; since I did not know
Whether thy bones had here their rest, or no.
But now 'tis known, behold; behold, I bring
Unto thy ghost, th' effused offering:
And look, what smallage, night-shade, cypress, yew,
Unto the shades have been, or now are due,
Here I devote; and something more than so;
I come to pay a debt of birth I owe.
Thou gav'st me life, (but mortal); for that one
Favour, I'll make full satisfaction;
For my life mortal, rise from out thy hearse,
And take a life immortal from my verse.

Delight in Disorder

A sweet disorder in the dress
Kindles in clothes a wantonness.
A lawn[2] about the shoulders thrown
Into a fine distraction;
An erring lace, which here and there
Enthralls the crimson stomacher;
A cuff neglectful, and thereby
Ribbands to flow confusedly;
A winning wave (deserving note)
In the tempestuous petticoat;
A careless shoestring, in whose tie
I see a wild civility—
Do more bewitch me than when art
Is too precise in every part.

---

[1]*luster*: five years. Herrick's father died when his son was 14 months old (1592).
[2]*lawn*: a fine linen used in dressmaking.

Dean Bourn, a Rude River in Devon, by Which Sometimes He Lived

Dean Bourn, farewell; I never look to see
Dean, or thy warty incivility.
Thy rocky bottom, that doth tear thy streams
And makes them frantic, ev'n to all extremes;
To my content, I never should behold,
Were thy streams silver, or thy rocks all gold.
Rocky thou art; and rocky we discover
Thy men; and rocky are thy ways all over.
O men, O manners; now, and ever known
To be a rocky generation!
A people currish; churlish as the seas;
And rude (almost) as rudest savages.
With whom I did, and may re-sojourn when
Rocks turn to rivers, rivers turn to men.

His Cavalier

Give me that man, that dares bestride
The active sea-horse, & with pride,
Through that huge field of waters ride:
Who, with his looks too, can appease
The ruffling winds and raging seas,
In midst of all their outrages.
This, this a virtuous man can do,
Sail against rocks, and split them too:
Ay! and a world of pikes pass through.

Julia Disdainful: or, The Frozen Zone

Whither? Say, whither shall I fly,
To slack these flames wherein I fry?
To the treasures, shall I go,
Of the rain, frost, hail, and snow?
Shall I search the underground,

Where all damps, and mists are found?
Shall I seek, for speedy ease,
All the floods, and frozen seas?
Or descend into the deep,
Where eternal cold does keep?
These may cool; but there's a zone
Colder yet than any one:
That's my Julia's breast; where dwells
Such destructive icicles,
As that the congealation will
Me sooner starve, than those can kill.

His Farewell to Sack[1]

Farewell thou thing, time-past so known, so dear
To me, as blood to life and spirit: near,
Nay, thou more near than kindred, friend, man, wife,
Male to the female, soul to body: life
To quick action, or the warm soft side
Of the resigning, yet resisting bride.
The kiss of virgins; first-fruits of the bed;
Soft speech, smooth touch, the lips, the maiden-head:
These, and a thousand sweets, could never be
So near, or dear, as thou wast once to me.
O thou the drink of gods, and angels! Wine
That scatter'st spirit and lust; whose purest shine,
More radiant than the summer's sun-beams shows;
Each way illustrious, brave; and like to those
Comets we see by night; whose shagg'd portents
Foretell the coming of some dire events:
Or some full flame, which with a pride aspires,
Throwing about his wild, and active fires.
'Tis thou, above nectar, O divinest soul!
(Eternal in thyself) that canst control
That, which subverts whole nature, grief and care;
Vexation of the mind, and damn'd despair.
'Tis thou, alone, who with thy mystic fan,[2]
Work'st more than wisdom, art, or nature can,

---

[1]*Sack*: strong Spanish white wine, favorite also of Shakespeare's Falstaff.
[2]*mystic fan*: the ceremonial fan borne in Bacchic processions.

To rouse the sacred madness; and awake
The frost-bound-blood, and spirits; and to make
Them frantic with thy raptures, flashing through
The soul, like lightning, and as active too.
'Tis not Apollo can, or those thrice three
Castalian sisters,[1] sing, if wanting thee.
Horace, Anacreon both had lost their fame,
Hadst thou not fill'd them with thy fire and flame.
Phœbean splendour! and thou Thespian spring!
Of which, sweet swans must drink, before they sing
Their true-pac'd-numbers, and their holy-lays,
Which makes them worthy cedar, and the bays.
But why? why longer do I gaze upon
Thee with the eye of admiration?
Since I must leave thee; and enforc'd, must say
To all thy witching beauties, Go, Away.
But if thy whimp'ring looks do ask me why?
Then know, that nature bids thee go, not I.
'Tis her erroneous self has made a brain
Uncapable of such a sovereign,
As is thy powerful self. Prithee not smile;
Or smile more inly; lest thy looks beguile
My vows denounc'd[2] in zeal, which thus much show thee,
That I have sworn, but by thy looks to know thee.
Let others drink thee freely; and desire
Thee and their lips espous'd; while I admire,
And love thee; but not taste thee. Let my Muse
Fail of thy former helps; and only use
Her inadult'rate strength: what's done by me
Hereafter, shall smell of the lamp, not thee.

The Vision

Sitting alone (as one forsook)
Close by a silver-shedding brook;
With hands held up to love, I wept;
And after sorrows spent, I slept:
Then in a vision I did see

---

[1]*Castalian sisters*: the nine Muses.
[2]*denounc'd*: proclaimed.

A glorious form appear to me:
A virgin's face she had; her dress
Was like a sprightly Spartaness.
A silver bow with green silk strung,
Down from her comely shoulders hung:
And as she stood, the wanton air
Dandled the ringlets of her hair.
Her legs were such Diana shows,
When tuck'd up she a-hunting goes;
With buskins short'ned to descry
The happy dawning of her thigh:
Which when I saw, I made access
To kiss that tempting nakedness:
But she forbad me, with a wand
Of myrtle she had in her hand:
And chiding me, said, Hence, Remove,
Herrick, thou art too coarse to love.

Upon a Black Twist Rounding the Arm of the Countess of Carlile

I saw about her spotless wrist,
Of blackest silk a curious twist;
Which, circumvolving gently, there
Enthrall'd her arm as prisoner.
Dark was the jail, but as if light
Had met t' engender with the night;
Or so as darkness made a stay
To show at once both night and day.
I fancy more! but if there be
Such freedom in captivity;
I beg of Love, that ever I
May in like chains of darkness lie.

On Himself

I fear no earthly powers;
But care for crowns of flowers:
And love to have my beard

With wine and oil besmear'd.
This day I'll drown all sorrow;
Who knows to live to-morrow?

Upon Julia's Petticoat

Thy azure robe, I did behold,
As airy as the leaves of gold;
Which erring here, and wand'ring there,
Pleas'd with transgression ev'rywhere.
Sometimes 'twould pant, and sigh, and heave,
As if to stir it scarce had leave:
But having got it, thereupon,
'Twould make a brave expansion;
And pounc'd[1] with stars, it show'd to me
Like a celestial canopy.
Sometimes 'twould blaze, and then abate,
Like to a flame grown moderate:
Sometimes away 'twould wildly fling,
Then to thy thighs so closely cling,
That some conceit did melt me down,
As lovers fall into a swoon;
And all confus'd, I there did lie
Drown'd in delights, but could not die.
That leading cloud, I followed still,
Hoping t' have seen of it my fill;
But ah! I could not: should it move
To life eternal, I could love.

To His Dying Brother, Master William Herrick

Life of my life, take not so soon thy flight,
But stay the time till we have bade Good night.
Thou hast both wind and tide with thee; thy way
As soon dispatch'd is by the night, as day.
Let us not then so rudely henceforth go

---

[1]*pounc'd*: sprinkled, as with powder.

Till we have wept, kiss'd, sighed, shook hands, or so.
There's pain in parting; and a kind of hell,
When once true-lovers take their last farewell.
What? shall we two our endless leaves take here
Without a sad look, or a solemn tear?
He knows not love, that hath not this truth proved,
Love is most loth to leave the thing beloved.
Pay we our vows, and go; yet when we part,
Then, even then, I will bequeath my heart
Into thy loving hands: for I'll keep none
To warm my breast, when thou my pulse art gone.
No, here I'll last, and walk (a harmless shade)
About this urn, wherein thy dust is laid,
To guard it so, as nothing here shall be
Heavy, to hurt those sacred seeds of thee.

The Welcome to Sack

So soft streams meet, so springs with gladder smiles
Meet after long divorcement by the isles;
When Love (the child of likeness) urgeth on
Their Crystal natures to an union.
So meet stol'n kisses, when the moony nights
Call forth fierce lovers to their wish'd delights:
So kings & queens meet, when desire convinces
All thoughts, but such as aim at getting princes,
As I meet thee. Soul of my life, and fame!
Eternal lamp of love! whose radiant flame
Out-glares the heav'ns' Osiris*; and thy gleams
Out-shine the splendour of his mid-day beams.
Welcome, O welcome my illustrious spouse;
Welcome as are the ends unto my vows:
Ay! far more welcome than the happy soil,
The sea-scourg'd merchant, after all his toil,
Salutes with tears of joy; when fires betray
The smoky chimneys of his Ithaca.
Where hast thou been so long from my embraces,
Poor pitied exile? Tell me, did thy Graces
Fly discontented hence, and for a time

---

*The Sun.

Did rather choose to bless another clime?
Or went'st thou to this end, the more to move me,
By thy short absence, to desire and love thee?
Why frowns my Sweet? Why won't my Saint confer
Favours on me, her fierce idolater?
Why are those looks, those looks the which have been
Time-past so fragrant, sickly now drawn in
Like a dull twilight? Tell me; and the fault
I'll expiate with sulphur, hair, and salt:[1]
And with the crystal humour[2] of the spring,
Purge hence the guilt, and kill this quarrelling.
Would thou not smile, or tell me what's amiss?
Have I been cold to hug thee, too remiss,
Too temp'rate in embracing? Tell me, has desire
To thee-ward died i' th' embers, and no fire
Left in this rak'd-up ash-heap, as a mark
To testify the glowing of a spark?
Have I divorc'd thee only to combine
In hot adult'ry with another wine?
True, I confess I left thee, and appeal
'Twas done by me, more to confirm my zeal,
And double my affection on thee; as do those,
Whose love grows more enflam'd, by being foes.
But to forsake thee ever, could there be
A thought of such like possibility?
When thou thyself dar'st say, thy isles shall lack
Grapes, before Herrick leaves Canary Sack.
Thou mak'st me airy, active to be borne,
Like Iphyclus, upon the tops of corn.
Thou mak'st me nimble, as the winged hours,[3]
To dance and caper on the heads of flowers,
And ride the sun-beams. Can there be a thing
Under the heavenly Isis*, that can bring
More love unto my life, or can present
My genius with a fuller blandishment?
Illustrious Idol! could th' Egyptians seek
Help from the garlic, onion, and the leek,
And pay no vows to thee? who wast their best

[1]*sulphur, hair, and salt*: (i.e. burnt) ceremonial rite of atonement.
[2]*crystal humour*: water.
[3]*hours*: Horae (goddesses of the seasons, attendant on Venus).
*The moon.

God, and far more transcendent than the rest?
Had Cassius,[1] that weak water-drinker, known
Thee in thy vine, or had but tasted one
Small chalice of thy frantic liquor; he
As the wise Cato[2] had approv'd of thee.
Had not Jove's son,* that brave Tyrinthian swain,
(Invited to the Thesbian banquet) ta'en
Full goblets of thy gen'rous blood; his spright
Ne'r had kept heat for fifty maids that night.
Come, come and kiss me; love and lust commends
Thee, and thy beauties; kiss, we will be friends,
Too strong for Fate to break us: look upon
Me, with that full pride of complexion,
As queens, meet queens; or come thou unto me,
As Cleopatra came to Anthony;
When her high carriage did at once present
To the triumvir, love and wonderment.
Swell up my nerves with spirit; let my blood
Run through my veins, like to a hasty flood.
Fill each part full of fire, active to do
What thy commanding soul shall put it to.
And till I turn Apostate to thy love,
Which here I vow to serve, do not remove
Thy fires from me; but Apollo's curse
Blast these-like actions, or a thing that's worse;
When these circumstants[3] shall but live to see
The time that I prevaricate from thee.
Call me *The Son of Beer*,[4] and then confine
Me to the tap, the toast, the turf;[5] let wine
Ne'r shine upon me; may my numbers all
Run to a sudden death, and funeral.
And last, when thee (dear spouse) I disavow,
Ne'r may prophetic Daphne crown my brow.

---

[1]*Cassius*: the co-conspirator, with Brutus, against Julius Caesar; a known tee-
    totaler.
[2]*Cato*: cf. note to "When He Would Have His Verses Read," p. 2.
*Hercules.
[3]*circumstants*: bystanders.
[4]*The Son of Beer*: instead of the "Son of Ben [Jonson]," nickname of the Cavaliers.
[5]*tap . . . turf*: beer, bread dipped in beer and earth (i.e. the clay as opposed to the
    firmament).

To Live Merrily, and to Trust to Good Verses

Now is the time for mirth,
    Nor cheek, or tongue be dumb:
For with the flow'ry earth,
    The golden pomp is come.

The golden pomp is come;
    For now each tree does wear
(Made of her pap and gum)
    Rich beads of amber here.

Now reigns the rose, and now
    Th' Arabian dew besmears
My uncontrolled brow,
    And my retorted hairs.

Homer, this health to thee,
    In sack of such a kind,
That it would make thee see,
    Though thou wert ne'r so blind.

Next, Virgil, I'll call forth,
    To pledge this second health
In wine, whose each cup's worth
    An Indian Common-wealth.

A goblet next I'll drink
    To Ovid; and suppose,
Made he the pledge, he'd think
    The world had all one Nose.[1]

Then this immensive cup
    Of aromatic wine,
Catullus, I quaff up
    To that terse muse of thine.

Wild I am now with heat;
    O Bacchus! cool thy rays!
Or frantic I shall eat
    Thy thyrse, and bite the bays.

---

[1]*Nose*: a pun on Ovid's family name, Naso, which suggests that Ovid had an
    ancestor with a remarkable nose.

Round, round, the roof does run;
   And being ravish'd thus,
Come, I will drink a tun
   To my Propertius.

Now, to Tibullus, next,
   This flood I drink to thee:
But stay; I see a text,
   That this presents to me.[1]

Behold, Tibullus lies
   Here burnt, whose small return
Of ashes, scarce suffice
   To fill a little urn.

Trust to good verses then;
   They only will aspire,
When pyramids, as men,
   Are lost, i' th' funeral fire.

And when all bodies meet
   In Lethe to be drown'd;
Then only numbers sweet,
   With endless life are crown'd.

To the Virgins, to Make Much of Time

Gather ye rose-buds while ye may,
   Old Time is still a-flying:
And this same flower that smiles to-day,
   To-morrow will be dying.

The glorious lamp of heaven, the sun,
   The higher he's a-getting;
The sooner will his race be run,
   And nearer he's to setting.

That age is best, which is the first,
   When youth and blood are warmer;
But being spent, the worse, and worst
   Times, still succeed the former.

---

[1]The next quatrain is a translation of two lines from Ovid's *Amores* (III. 9, 39–40).

Then be not coy, but use your time;
   And while ye may, go marry:
For having lost but once your prime,
   You may for ever tarry.

Her Legs

I fain would kiss my Julia's dainty leg,
Which is as white and hairless as an egg.

Chop-Cherry

1.

Thou gav'st me leave to kiss;
Thou gav'st me leave to woo;
Thou mad'st me think by this,
And that, thou lov'dst me too.

2.

But I shall ne'r forget,
How for to make thee merry;
Thou mad'st me chop, but yet,
Another snapp'd the cherry.

To Dianeme

Show me thy feet, show me thy legs, thy thighs,
Show me those fleshy principalities;
Show me that hill where smiling love doth sit,
Having a living fountain under it;
Show me thy waist: then let me therewithal,
By the ascension of thy lawn, see all.

Putrefaction

Putrefaction is the end
Of all that Nature doth intend.

Ill Government

Preposterous is that government, (and rude)
When Kings obey the wilder Multitude.

To Marygolds

Give way, and be ye ravish'd by the sun,
(And hang the head whenas the act is done)
Spread as he spreads; wax less as he does wane;
And as he shuts, close up to maids again.

His Content in the Country

Here, here I live with what my board,
Can with the smallest cost afford.
Though ne'r so mean the viands be,
They well content my Prue[1] and me.
Or pea, or bean, or wort, or beet,
What ever comes, content makes sweet:
Here we rejoice, because no rent
We pay for our poor tenement:
Wherein we rest, and never fear
The landlord, or the usurer.
The quarter-day does ne'r affright
Our peaceful slumbers in the night.
We eat our own, and batten more,
Because we feed on no man's score:
But pity those, whose flanks grow great,

[1]*Prue*: Herrick's housekeeper, Prudence Baldwin.

Swell'd with the lard of others' meat.
We bless our fortunes, when we see
Our own beloved privacy:
And like our living, where w' are known
To very few, or else to none.

Life Is the Body's Light

Life is the body's light; which once declining,
Those crimson clouds i' th' cheeks & lips leave shining.
Those counter-changed tabbies in the air,
(The sun once set) all of one colour are.
So, when death comes, fresh tinctures lose their place,
And dismal darkness then doth smutch the face.

In the Dark None Dainty

Night hides our thefts; all faults then pardon'd be:
All are alike fair, when no spots we see.
Lais and Lucrece, in the night time are
Pleasing alikc; alike both singular:
Joan and my lady havé at that time one,
One and the self-same priz'd complexion.
Then please alike the pewter and the plate;
The chosen ruby, and the reprobate.[1]

Upon the Troublesome Times

1.

O! Times most bad,
Without the scope
　　Of hope
Of better to be had!

---

[1]*reprobate*: flawed gem.

2.

Where shall I go,
Or whither run
    To shun
This public overthrow?

3.

No places are
(This I am sure)
    Secure
In this our wasting war.

4.

Some storms w'ave past;
Yet we must all
    Down fall,
And perish at the last.

The Bad Season Makes the Poet Sad

Dull to myself, and almost dead to these
My many fresh and fragrant mistresses:
Lost to all music now; since every thing
Puts on the semblance here of sorrowing.
Sick is the land to' th' heart; and doth endure
More dangerous faintings by her desp'rate cure.
But if that golden age would come again,
And Charles here rule, as he before did reign;
If smooth and unperplex'd the seasons were,
As when the sweet Maria[1] lived here:
I should delight to have my curls half drown'd
In Tyrian dews, and head with roses crown'd.
And once more yet (ere I am laid out dead)
Knock at a star with my exalted head.

---

[1]*sweet Maria*: Charles's queen, Henrietta-Maria Bourbon (1609–1669), sister of
    Louis XIII.

What Kind of Mistress He Would Have

Be the mistress of my choice
Clean in manners, clear in voice;
Be she witty, more than wise;
Pure enough, though not precise:[1]
Be she showing in her dress,
Like a civil wilderness;
That the curious may detect
Order in a sweet neglect:
Be she rowling in her eye,
Tempting all the passers by;
And each ringlet of her hair
An enchantment, or a snare
For to catch the lookers-on,
But herself held fast by none.
Let her Lucrece[2] all day be,
Thaïs[3] in the night, to me.
Be she such, as neither will
Famish me, nor over-fill.

To Fortune

Tumble me down, and I will sit
Upon my ruins (smiling yet);
Tear me to tatters; yet I'll be
Patient in my necessity.
Laugh at my scraps of clothes, and shun
Me, as a fear'd infection:
Yet scarecrow-like I'll walk, as one,
Neglecting thy derision.

---

[1]*precise*: over-virtuous.
[2]*Lucrece*: in Roman lore the wife of Tarquinius Collatinus. After her rape by
Sextus Tarquinius, she committed suicide.
[3]*Thaïs*: Athenian courtesan (4th century B.C.); mistress of Alexander the Great,
later of the king of Egypt.

Cruelties

Nero commanded; but withdrew his eyes
From the beholding Death, and cruelties.

The May-pole

    The May-pole is up,
    Now give me the cup;
I'll drink to the garlands around it:
    But first unto those
    Whose hands did compose
The glory of flowers that crown'd it.

    A health to my girls,
    Whose husbands may Earls
Or Lords be, (granting my wishes)
    And when that ye wed
    To the bridal bed,
Then multiply all, like to fishes.

Love Palpable

I press'd my Julia's lips, and in the kiss
Her Soul and Love were palpable in this.

His Grange, or Private Wealth

      Though clock,
To tell how night draws hence, I've none,
      A cock,
I have, to sing how day draws on.
      I have
A maid (my Prue) by good luck sent,
      To save
That little, Fates me gave or lent.
      A hen

I keep, which creeking day by day,
   Tells when
She goes her long white egg to lay.
   A goose
I have, which, with a jealous ear,
   Lets loose
Her tongue, to tell what danger's near.
   A lamb
I keep (tame) with my morsels fed,
   Whose dam
An orphan left him (lately dead).
   A cat
I keep, that plays about my house,
   Grown fat,
With eating many a miching mouse.
   To these
A Trasy* I do keep, whereby
   I please
The more my rural privacy:
   Which are
But toys, to give my heart some ease:
   Where care
None is, slight things do lightly please.

Upon Julia's Clothes

Whenas in silks my Julia goes,
Then, then (me thinks) how sweetly flows
That liquefaction of her clothes.

Next, when I cast mine eyes and see
That brave vibration each way free;
O how that glittering taketh me!

---

*His Spaniel.

To His Honoured and Most Ingenious Friend Mr. Charles Cotton[1]

For brave comportment, wit without offence,
Words fully flowing, yet of influence:
Thou art that man of men, the man alone,
Worthy the public admiration:
Who with thine own eyes read'st what we do write,
And giv'st our numbers euphony, and weight.
Tell'st when a verse springs high, how understood
To be, or not born of the Royal blood.
What state above, what symmetry below,
Lines have, or should have, thou the best canst show.
For which (my Charles) it is my pride to be,
Not so much known, as to be lov'd of thee.
Long may I live so, and my wreath of bays,
Be less another's laurel, than thy praise.

Anacreontic[2]

I must
Not trust
Here to any;
Bereav'd,
Deceiv'd
By so many:
As one
Undone
By my losses;
Comply
Will I
With my crosses.
Yet still
I will

---

[1]*Charles Cotton*: generally considered to be Charles Cotton the elder (d. 1658), a gentleman whose wit and bonhomie are also praised in Lovelace's "The Grasshopper" (page 74 of this volume). He is often confused with his son of the same name (1630–1687), who was a poet of some distinction.
[2]*Anacreontic*: in the manner of the Greek poet Anacreon (572?–?488 B.C.).

Not be grieving;
    Since thence
    And hence
Comes relieving.
    But this
    Sweet is
In our mourning;
    Times bad
    And sad
Are a-turning:
    And he
    Whom we
See dejected;
    Next day
    We may
See erected.

To the King

Upon His Taking of Leicester[1]

This day is yours, Great CHARLES! and in this war
Your fate, and ours, alike victorious are.
In her white stole; now Victory does rest
Enspher'd with palm on your triumphant crest.
Fortune is now your captive; other kings
Hold but her hands; you hold both hands and wings.

Kisses Loathsome

I abhor the slimy kiss,
(Which to me most loathsome is.)
Those lips please me which are plac'd
Close, but not too strictly lac'd:
Yielding I would have them; yet
Not a wimbling tongue admit:
What should poking-sticks make there,
When the ruff is set elsewhere?

---

[1]Charles marched on and decisively took Leicester in the spring of 1645 (leading
    directly to the hard-fought Battle of Naseby, at which Cromwell's New Model
    Army won an important victory).

The Present Time Best Pleaseth

Praise they that will times past, I joy to see
Myself now live: this age best pleaseth me.

His Answer to a Friend

You ask me what I do, and how I live?
And (noble friend) this answer I must give:
Drooping, I draw on to the vaults of death,
O'er which you'll walk, when I am laid beneath.

On Himself

I will no longer kiss,
I can no longer stay;
The way of all flesh is,
That I must go this day:
Since longer I can't live,
My frolic youths, adieu;
My lamp to you I'll give,
And all my troubles too.

His Last Request to Julia

I have been wanton, and too bold I fear,
To chafe o'er much the virgin's cheek or ear.
Beg for my pardon, Julia; he doth win
Grace with the gods who's sorry for his sin.
That done, my Julia, dearest Julia, come,
And go with me to choose my burial room.
My fates are ended; when thy Herrick dies,
Clasp thou his book, then close thou up his eyes.

The Pillar of Fame

Fame's pillar here, at last, we set,
Out-during marble, brass, or jet,
Charm'd and enchanted so,
As to withstand the blow
Of   overthrow:
Nor shall the seas,
Or   OUTRAGES
Of storms o'erbear
What we up-rear,
ThoKingdomsfal,
This   pillar   never   shall
Decline   or   waste   at   all;
But stand for ever by his own
Firm and well fix'd foundation.

To his book's end this last line he'd have plac'd,
Jocund his Muse was; but his Life was chaste.[1]

His Prayer for Absolution

For those my unbaptized rhymes,
Writ in my wild unhallowed times;
For every sentence, clause and word,
That's not inlaid with Thee (my Lord)
Forgive me God, and blot each line
Out of my book, that is not Thine.
But if, 'mongst all, thou find'st here one
Worthy thy benediction;
That one of all the rest, shall be
The glory of my work, and me.

---

[1]This couplet appeared at the end of *Hesperides*. The following poems by Herrick are from his religious volume *Noble Numbers* (1648).

A Thanksgiving to God, for His House

Lord, Thou hast given me a cell
      Wherein to dwell;
A little house, whose humble roof
      Is weather-proof;
Under the spars of which I lie
      Both soft, and dry;
Where Thou my chamber for to ward
      Hast set a guard
Of harmless thoughts, to watch and keep
      Me, while I sleep.
Low is my porch, as is my Fate,
      Both void of state;
And yet the threshold of my door
      Is worn by th' poor,
Who thither come, and freely get
      Good words, or meat:
Like as my parlour, so my hall
      And kitchen's small:
A little buttery, and therein
      A little bin,
Which keeps my little loaf of bread
      Unchipp'd, unflead:[1]
Some brittle sticks of thorn or briar
      Make me a fire,
Close by whose living coal I sit,
      And glow like it.
Lord, I confess too, when I dine,
      The pulse is Thine,
And all those other bits, that be
      There plac'd by Thee;
The worts, the purslane, and the mess
      Of watercress,
Which of Thy kindness Thou hast sent;
      And my content
Makes those, and my beloved beet,
      To be more sweet.

---

[1]*Unchipp'd, unflead*: unvisited by vermin or mold.

'Tis Thou that crown'st my glittering hearth
       With guiltless mirth;
And giv'st me wassail bowls to drink,
       Spic'd to the brink.
Lord, 'tis thy plenty-dropping hand,
       That soils my land;
And giv'st me, for my bushel sown,
       Twice ten for one:
Thou mak'st my teeming hen to lay
       Her egg each day:
Besides my healthful ewes to bear
       Me twins each year:
The while the conduits of my kine
       Run cream, (for wine).
All these, and better Thou dost send
       Me, to this end,
That I should render, for my part,
       A thankful heart;
Which, fir'd with incense, I resign,
       As wholly Thine;
But the acceptance, that must be,
       My Christ, by Thee.

Eternity

1.

O Years! and Age! Farewell:
    Behold I go,
    Where I do know
Infinity to dwell.

2.

And these mine eyes shall see
    All times, how they
    Are lost i' th' sea
Of vast eternity.

3.

Where never moon shall sway
    The stars; but she,
    And night, shall be
Drown'd in one endless day.

To Christ

I crawl, I creep; my Christ, I come
To Thee, for curing balsamum:
Thou hast, nay more, Thou art the tree,
Affording salve of sovereignty.
My mouth I'll lay unto Thy wound
Bleeding, that no blood touch the ground:
For, rather than one drop shall fall
To waste, my JESU, I'll take all.

Salutation

Christ, I have read, did to His chaplains say,
Sending them forth, *Salute no man by th' way:*
Not that He taught His ministers to be
Unsmooth, or sour to all civility;
But to instruct them, to avoid all snares
Of tardidation in the Lord's affairs.
Manners are good: but till his errand ends,
Salute we must, nor strangers, kin, or friends.

Christ's Sadness

Christ was not sad, i' th' garden, for His own
Passion, but for his sheeps' dispersion.

To God

Come to me God; but do not come
To me, as to the gen'ral doom,
In power; or come Thou in that state,
When Thou Thy laws didst promulgate,
When as the mountains quak'd for dread,
And sullen clouds bound up his head.
No, lay thy stately terrors by,

To talk with me familiarly;
For if Thy thunder-claps I hear,
I shall less swoon, than die for fear.
Speak thou of love and I'll reply
By way of epithalamy,[1]
Or sing of mercy, and I'll suit
To it my viol and my lute:
Thus let Thy lips but love distil,
Then come my God, and hap what will.

The Right Hand

God has a right hand, but is quite bereft
Of that, which we do nominate the left.

His Anthem, to Christ on the Cross

　　　　When I behold Thee, almost slain,
　　　　With one, and all parts, full of pain:
　　　　When I Thy gentle heart do see
　　　　Pierc'd through, and dropping blood, for me,
　　　　I'll call, and cry out, Thanks to Thee.

Vers.　　But yet it wounds my soul, to think,
　　　　That for my sin, Thou, Thou must drink,
　　　　Even Thou alone, the bitter cup
　　　　Of fury, and of vengeance up.

Chor.　　Lord, I'll not see Thee to drink all
　　　　The vinegar, the myrrh, the gall:

Ver. Chor.　But I will sip a little wine;
　　　　Which done, Lord say, The rest is mine.

---

[1]*Epithalamy*: variant of *epithalamium*, an ode in honor of a wedding.

The Cross-tree

This   cross-tree   here
Doth   JESUS   bear,
Who   sweet'ned   first,
The   death   accurs'd.
Here all things ready are, make haste, make haste away;
For, long this work will be, & very short this day.
Why then, go on to act: here's wonders to be done,
Before the last least sand of Thy ninth hour be run;
Or ere dark clouds do dull, or dead the mid-day's sun.

Act   when   Thou   wilt,
Blood   will   be   spilt;
Pure   balm,   that   shall
Bring   health   to   all.
Why   then,   begin
To   pour   first   in
Some   drops   of   wine,
In   stead   of   brine,
To search the wound,
So   long   unsound:
And, when that's done,
Let   oil,   next,   run,
To   cure   the   sore
Sin   made   before.
And O! Dear Christ,
E'en   as   Thou   di'st,
Look   down,   and   see
Us   weep   for   Thee.
And tho (love knows)
Thy   dreadful   woes
We   cannot   ease;
Yet   do   Thou   please,
Who   mercy   art,
T'accept   each   heart,
That   gladly   would
Help,   if   it   could.
Meanwhile,   let   me,
Beneath   this   tree,
This   honour   have,
To   make   my   grave.

THOMAS CAREW

THOMAS CAREW (1595?–?1639) began his professional career as an assistant to the English ambassador to the Netherlands in 1616. He was dismissed that same year, apparently for making insulting remarks to the ambassador and his wife. After a more successful period in an embassy to the French court, he returned to England and in 1628 was made a gentleman of Charles I's Privy Chamber. There, he was, it is said, "high in favour with that king, who had a high opinion of his wit and abilities."[1]

Carew (whose name is pronounced Carey) had a reputation for mischief and debauchery that stayed with him all of his adult life. But the reputation was not at all damaging to his career as a poet, soldier and court gentleman. His society verses were very popular, prized especially for their petulant wit. In such pieces as "A Divine Mistress" and "Disdain Returned," Carew could execute deftly the amorous parry or riposte. And, with "To Saxham," he made an important contribution to the seventeenth-century genre of poems about country houses, an important aspect of the Cavalier poet's repertoire. Gentry who entertained royalty or nobility, or simply a poet, with hunting, feasting and socializing were repaid in sumptuous lines praising their generosity and spreading the fame of their household. Perhaps the best-known such poem of the age is Ben Jonson's "To Penshurst" (1616). Saxham was a house owned by a Sir John Crofts (1563–1628), whose qualities as a host were famous and often apostrophized by poets, and who more than once lodged King Charles. Carew also composed an elegy for Sir John's granddaughter Maria. And there is yet another side to Carew's poetry. In "An Elegy on the Death of . . . Dr. John Donne," the poet composed probably the finest elegy of the period. Flawless in its dignified, solemn pace, it is also a wonderfully astute appraisal of that elder poet's contribution to English poetry and (Carew stresses) the English language.

At the end of his life, Carew attempted to make amends to the Church, summoning a prominent vicar to his deathbed. Owing to his profligate life, however, he was repulsed. He also began a set of verse translations of the Psalms, which survive but are generally thought to be inferior. Outshining these failures, however, is the work of one of the truly finest English poets of the seventeenth century.

---

[1] *The Dictionary of National Biography*, Oxford University Press, London, 1917 ff., Volume III, page 972.

The Spring

Now that the Winter's gone, the earth hath lost
Her snow-white robes, and now no more the frost
Candies the grass, or casts an icy cream
Upon the silver lake or crystal stream:
But the warm sun thaws the benumbed earth,
And makes it tender, gives a sacred birth
To the dead swallow; wakes in hollow tree
The drowsy cuckoo and the humble-bee.
Now do a choir of chirping minstrels bring
In triumph to the world the youthful Spring:
The valleys, hills, and woods in rich array
Welcome the coming of the long'd-for May.
Now all things smile: only my love doth lour,
Nor hath the scalding noonday sun the power
To melt that marble ice which still doth hold
Her heart congeal'd, and makes her pity cold.
The ox, which lately did for shelter fly
Into the stall, doth now securely lie
In open fields; and love no more is made
By the fireside, but in the cooler shade
Amyntas now doth with his Chloris sleep
Under a sycamore, and all things keep
    Time with the season: only she doth carry
    June in her eyes, in her heart January.

Good Counsel to a Young Maid

Gaze not on thy beauty's pride,
Tender maid, in the false tide
That from lovers' eyes doth slide.

Let thy faithful crystal show,
How thy colours come, and go,
Beauty takes a foil from woe.

Love, that in those smooth streams lies,
Under pity's fair disguise,
Will thy melting heart surprise.

Nets, of passion's finest thread,
Snaring poems, will be spread
All, to catch thy maiden-head.

Then beware, for those that cure
Love's disease, themselves endure
For reward a calenture.

Rather let the lover pine,
Than his pale cheek should assign
A perpetual blush to thine.

The Inscription on the Tomb of the Lady Mary Wentworth

MARIA WENTWORTH, *Thomae Comitis Cleveland, filia prae-mortua prima virginiam animam exhaluit. An. Dom. 1632 Æt. suae 18.*[1]

And here the precious dust is laid;
Whose purely-tempered clay was made
So fine, that it the guest betray'd.

Else the soul grew so fast within,
It broke the outward shell of sin,
And so was hatch'd a cherubin.

In height, it soar'd to God above;
In depth, it did to knowledge move,
And spread in breadth to general love.

Before, a pious duty shin'd
To parents, courtesy behind,
On either side an equal mind.

Good to the poor, to kindred dear,
To servants kind, to friendship clear,
To nothing but herself severe.

So though a virgin, yet a bride
To every grace, she justified
A chaste poligamy, and died.

---

[1]*Thomae*, etc.: "First daughter of Thomas Earl of Cleveland, prematurely dead, gave up her virgin soul in 1632 at age 18."

Learn from hence (reader) what small trust
We owe this world, where virtue must
Frail as our flesh crumble to dust.

An Elegy upon the Death of the Dean of St. Paul's, Dr. John Donne

Can we not force from widowed poetry,
Now thou art dead (Great DONNE), one elegy
To crown thy hearse? Why yet dare we not trust
Though with unkneaded dough-bak'd prose thy dust,
Such as the unscissor'd churchman from the flower
Of fading rhetoric, short liv'd as his hour,
Dry as the sand that measures it, should lay
Upon thy ashes, on the funeral day?
Have we no voice, no tune? Did'st thou dispense
Through all our language, both the words and sense?
'Tis a sad truth; the pulpit may her plain,
And sober Christian precepts still retain,
Doctrines it may, and wholesome uses frame,
Grave homilies, and lectures, but the flame
Of thy brave soul, that shot such heat and light,
As burnt our earth, and made our darkness bright,
Committed holy rapes upon our will,
Did through the eye the melting heart distil;
And the deep knowledge of dark truths so teach,
As sense might judge, what fancy could not reach,
Must be desir'd for ever. So the fire,
That fills with spirit and heat the Delphic choir,
Which kindled first by thy Promethean breath,
Glow'd here a while, lies quench'd now in thy death;
The Muses' garden with pedantic weeds
O'erspread, was purg'd by thee; the lazy seeds
Of servile imitation thrown away,
And fresh invention planted, thou didst pay
The debts of our penurious bankrupt age;
Licentious thefts, that make poetic rage
A mimic fury, when our souls must be
Possess'd or with Anacreon's extasy,
Or Pindar's, not their own; the subtle cheat
Of sly exchanges, and the juggling feat

Of two-edg'd words, or whatsoever wrong
By ours was done the Greek, or Latin tongue,
Thou hast redeem'd, and open'd us a mine
Of rich and pregnant fancy, drawn a line
Of masculine expression, which had good
Old Orpheus seen, or all the ancient brood
Our superstitious fools admire, and hold
Their lead more precious than thy burnish'd gold,
Thou hadst been their exchequer, and no more
They each in others dust had rak'd for ore.
Thou shalt yield no precedence, but of time,
And the blind fate of language, whose tun'd chime
More charms the outward sense; yet thou may'st claim
From so great disadvantage greater fame,
Since to the awe of thy imperious wit
Our stubborn language bends, made only fit
With her tough-thick-ribb'd hoops to gird about
Thy giant fancy, which had prov'd too stout
For their soft melting phrases. As in time
They had the start, so did they cull the prime
Buds of invention many a hundred year,
And left the rifled fields, besides the fear
To touch their harvest, yet from those bare lands
Of what is purely thine, thy only hands
(And that thy smallest work) have gleaned more
Than all those times, and tongues could reap before;
But thou art gone, and thy strict laws will be
Too hard for libertines in poetry.
They will repeal the goodly exil'd train
Of gods and goddesses, which in thy just reign
Were banish'd nobler poems, now, with these
The silenc'd tales o' th' Metamorphoses
Shall stuff their lines, and swell the windy page,
Till verse refin'd by thee, in this last age
Turn ballad rhyme, or those old idols be
Ador'd again, with new apostasy;
Oh, pardon me, that break with untun'd verse
The reverend silence that attends thy hearse,
Whose awful solemn murmurs were to thee
More than these faint lines, a loud elegy,
That did proclaim in a dumb eloquence
The death of all the Arts, whose influence
Grown feeble, in these panting numbers lies
Gasping short winded accents, and so dies:

So doth the swiftly turning wheel not stand
In th'instant we withdraw the moving hand,
But some small time maintain a faint weak course
By virtue of the first impulsive force:
And so whil'st I cast on thy funeral pile
Thy crown of bays, oh, let it crack a while,
And spit disdain, till the devouring flashes
Suck all the moisture up, then turn to ashes.
I will not draw thee envy to engross
All thy perfections, or weep all our loss;
Those are too numerous for an elegy,
And this too great, to be express'd by me,
Though every pen should share a distinct part.
Yet art thou theme enough to tire all Art;
Let others carve the rest, it shall suffice
I on thy tombe this epitaph incise:

> Here lies a King, that rul'd as he thought fit
> The universal Monarchy of wit;
> Here lie two flamens,[1] and both those the best,
> Apollo's first, at last, the true God's Priest.

Boldness in Love

Mark how the bashful morn in vain
   Courts the amorous marigold,
With sighing blasts and weeping rain,
   Yet she refuses to unfold.
But when the planet of the day
Approacheth with his powerful ray,
Then she spreads, then she receives
His warmer beams into her virgin leaves.

So shalt thou thrive in love, fond boy;
   If thy tears and sighs discover
Thy grief, thou never shalt enjoy
   The just reward of a bold lover.
But when with moving accents thou
Shalt constant faith and service vow,
Thy Celia shall receive those charms
With open ears, and with unfolded arms.

---

[1]*flamen*: priest of a Roman deity, here Apollo.

A Divine Mistress

In Nature's pieces still I see
Some error that might mended be;
Something my wish could still remove,
Alter or add; but my fair love
Was fram'd by hands far more divine,
For she hath every beauteous line:
Yet I had been far happier,
Had Nature, that made me, made her.
Then likeness might (that love creates)
Have made her love what now she hates;
Yet I confess I cannot spare
From her just shape the smallest hair;
Nor need I beg from all the store
Of heaven for her one beauty more.
She hath too much divinity for me:
You gods, teach her some more humanity.

A Beautiful Mistress

If, when the sun at noon displays
          His brighter rays,
       Thou but appear,
He then, all pale with shame and fear,
          Quencheth his light,
Hides his dark brow, flies from thy sight,
       And grows more dim,
   Compar'd to thee, than stars to him.
If thou but show thy face again,
When darkness doth at midnight reign,
The darkness flies, and light is hurl'd
Round about the silent world:
So as alike thou driv'st away
Both light and darkness, night and day.

A Cruel Mistress

We read of kings and gods that kindly took
A pitcher fill'd with water from the brook;
But I have daily tend'red without thanks
Rivers of tears that overflow their banks.
A slaughter'd bull will appease angry Jove,
A horse the Sun, a lamb the God of Love;
But she disdains the spotless sacrifice
Of a pure heart, that at her altar lies.
Vesta is not displeas'd if her chaste urn[1]
Do with repaired fuel ever burn;
But my saint frowns, though to her honour'd name
I consecrate a never-dying flame.
Th' Assyrian king did none i' th' furnace throw[2]
But those that to his image did not bow;
With bended knees I daily worship her,
Yet she consumes her own idolater.
Of such a goddess no times leave record,
That burnt the temple where she was ador'd.

Song

To My Inconstant Mistress

When thou, poor excommunicate
    From all the joys of love, shalt see
The full reward, and glorious fate,
    Which my strong faith shall purchase me,
    Then curse thine own inconstancy.

A fairer hand than thine, shall cure
    That heart, which thy false oaths did wound;
And to my soul, a soul more pure
    Than thine, shall by Love's hand be bound,
    And both with equal glory crown'd.

---

[1]*Vesta*: Roman goddess of the hearth.
[2]*Assyrian king*: Nebuchadnezzar, who was actually Babylonian.

Then shalt thou weep, entreat, complain
 To Love, as I did once to thee;
When all thy tears shall be as vain
  As mine were then, for thou shalt be
  Damn'd for thy false Apostasy.

A *Prayer to the Wind*

Go thou gentle whispering wind,
Bear this sigh; and if thou find
Where my cruel fair doth rest,
Cast it in her snowy breast,
So, enflam'd by my desire,
It may set her heart a-fire.
Those sweet kisses thou shalt gain,
Will reward thee for thy pain:
Boldly light upon her lip,
There suck odours, and thence skip
To her bosom; lastly fall
Down, and wander over all:
Range about those ivory hills,
From whose every part distills
Amber dew; there spices grow,
There pure streams of nectar flow;
There perfume thyself, and bring
All those sweets upon thy wing:
As thou return'st, change by thy power,
Every weed into a flower;
Turn each thistle to a vine,
Make the bramble eglantine.
For so rich a booty made,
Do but this, and I am paid.
Thou canst with thy powerful blast,
Heat apace, and cool as fast:
Thou canst kindle hidden flame,
And again destroy the same;
Then for pity, either stir
Up the fire of love in her,
That alike both flames may shine,
Or else quite extinguish mine.

A Deposition from Love

I was foretold your rebel sex
  Nor love nor pity knew;
And with what scorn you use to vex
  Poor hearts that humbly sue.
Yet I believ'd, to crown our pain,
  Could we the fortress win,
The happy lover sure should gain
  A paradise within:
I thought Love's plagues, like dragons, sate
Only to fright us at the gate.

But I did enter, and enjoy
  What happy lovers prove;
For I could kiss, and sport, and toy,
  And taste those sweets of love,
Which, had they but a lasting state,
  Or if in Celia's breast
The force of love might not abate,
  Jove were too mean a guest:
But now her breach of faith far more
Afflicts, than did her scorn before.

Hard fate! to have been once possess'd,
  As victor, of a heart;
Achiev'd with labour and unrest,
  And then forc'd to depart.
If the stout foe will not resign,
  When I besiege a town,
I lose but what was never mine;
  But he that is cast down
From enjoy'd beauty, feels a woe
Only deposed kings can know.

Ingrateful Beauty Threat'ned

Know, Celia, since thou art so proud,
  'Twas I that gave thee thy renown;
Thou hadst in the forgotten crowd
  Of common beauties liv'd unknown,

Had not my verse exhal'd thy name,
And with it imp'd the wings of fame.[1]

That killing power is none of thine:
    I gave it to thy voice and eyes;
Thy sweets, thy graces, all are mine;
    Thou art my star, shin'st in my skies:
Then dart not from thy borrow'd sphere
Lightning on him that fix'd thee there.

Tempt me with such affrights no more,
    Lest what I made I uncreate;
Let fools thy mystic forms adore,
    I'll know thee in thy mortal state.
Wise poets that wrapp'd Truth in tales
Knew her themselves through all her veils.

Epitaph on the Lady Mary Villers

The Lady Mary Villers lies
Under this stone; with weeping eyes
The parents that first gave her birth,
And their sad friends, laid her in earth.
If any of them, Reader, were
Known unto thee, shed a tear;
Or if thyself possess a gem
As dear to thee, as this to them,
Though a stranger to this place,
Bewail in theirs thine own hard case:
For thou, perhaps, at thy return
May'st find thy darling in an urn.

Another

The purest soul that e'er was sent
Into a clayey tenement
Inform'd this dust; but the weak mould
Could the great guest no longer hold:

---

[1] *imp'd*: "imp" is a falconing term meaning "to repair by grafting on a feather."

The substance was too pure, the flame
Too glorious that thither came;
Ten thousand Cupids brought along
A grace on each wing, that did throng
For place there, till they all oppress'd
The seat in which they sought to rest:
So the fair model broke, for want
Of room to lodge th' inhabitant.

Another

This little vault, this narrow room,
Of love and beauty is the tomb;
The dawning beam that gan to clear
Our clouded sky lies dark'ned here,
For ever set to us, by death
Sent to inflame the world beneath.
'Twas but a bud, yet did contain
More sweetness than shall spring again;
A budding star, that might have grown
Into a sun when it had blown.
This hopeful beauty did create
New life in Love's declining state;
But now his empire ends, and we
From fire and wounding darts are free;
His brand, his bow, let no man fear:
The flames, the arrows, all lie here.

Song

Ask me no more where Jove bestows,
When June is past, the fading rose;
For in your beauty's orient deep
These flowers, as in their causes, sleep.

Ask me no more whither doth stray
The golden atoms of the day;
For in pure love heaven did prepare
Those powders to enrich your hair.

Ask me no more whither doth haste
The nightingale, when May is past;
For in your sweet dividing throat
She winters, and keeps warm her note.

Ask me no more where those stars light,
That downwards fall in dead of night;
For in your eyes they sit, and there
Fixed become as in their sphere.

Ask me no more if east or west
The phœnix builds her spicy nest;
For unto you at last she flies,
And in your fragrant bosom dies.

Disdain Returned

He that loves a rosy cheek,
    Or a coral lip admires,
Or from star-like eyes doth seek
    Fuel to maintain his fires;
As old Time makes these decay,
So his flames must waste away.

But a smooth and steadfast mind,
    Gentle thoughts and calm desires,
Hearts with equal love combin'd,
    Kindle never-dying fires.
Where these are not, I despise
Lovely cheeks, or lips, or eyes.

No tears, Celia, now shall win
    My resolv'd heart to return;
I have search'd thy soul within,
    And find naught but pride and scorn:
I have learn'd thy arts, and now
Can disdain as much as thou.
    Some power, in my revenge, convey
    That love to her I cast away.

To Celia, upon Love's Ubiquity

As one that strives, being sick, and sick to death,
By changing places to preserve a breath,
A tedious restless breath, removes, and tries
A thousand rooms, a thousand policies,
To cozen pain, when he thinks to find ease,
At last he finds all change but his disease;
So, like a ball with fire and powder fill'd,
I restless am, yet live, each minute kill'd,
And with that moving torture must retain,
With change of all things else, a constant pain.
Say I stay with you, presence is to me
Naught but a light to show my misery;
And partings are as racks to plague love on,
The further stretch'd, the more affliction.
Go I to Holland, France, or furthest Ind,
I change but only countries, not my mind;
And though I pass through air and water free,
Despair and hopeless fate still follow me.
Whilst in the bosom of the waves I reel,
My heart I'll liken to the tottering keel,
The sea to my own troubled fate, the wind
To your disdain, sent from a soul unkind.
But when I lift my sad looks to the skies,
Then shall I think I see my Celia's eyes;
And when a cloud or storm appears between,
I shall remember what her frowns have been.
Thus, whatsoever course my Fates allow,
All things but make me mind my business, you.
The good things that I meet, I think streams be
From you, the fountain; but when bad I see,
How vile and cursed is that thing, think I,
That to such goodness is so contrary!
My whole life is 'bout you, the centre star,
But a perpetual motion circular.
I am the dial's hand, still walking round,
You are the compass: and I never sound
Beyond your circle, neither can I show
Aught but what first expressed is in you:
That, wheresoever my tears do cause me move,
My fate still keeps me bounded with your love;
Which, ere it die, or be extinct in me,

Time shall stand still, and moist waves flaming be.
Yet, being gone, think not on me: I am
A thing too wretched for thy thoughts to name:
But when I die, and wish all comforts given,
I'll think on you, and by you think on heaven.

Celia Bleeding, to the Surgeon

Fond man, that canst believe her blood
   Will from those purple channels flow;
Or that the pure untainted flood
   Can any foul distemper know;
Or that thy weak steel can incise
The crystal case wherein it lies:

Know, her quick blood, proud of his seat,
   Runs dancing through her azure veins;
Whose harmony no cold nor heat
   Disturbs, whose hue no tincture stains:
And the hard rock wherein it dwells
The keenest darts of love repels.

But thou repli'st, "Behold, she bleeds!"
   Fool! thou 'rt deceiv'd, and dost not know
The mystic knot whence this proceeds,
   How lovers in each other grow:
Thou struck'st her arm, but 'twas my heart
Shed all the blood, felt all the smart.

To Saxham[1]

Though frost and snow lock'd from mine eyes
That beauty which without door lies,
Thy gardens, orchards, walks, that so
I might not all thy pleasures know;
Yet (Saxham) thou within thy gate
Art of thyself so delicate,

---

[1]*Saxham*: cf. introduction to Carew section.

So full of native sweets, that bless
Thy roof with inward happiness,
As neither from nor to thy store
Winter takes aught, or Spring adds more.
The cold and frozen air had starv'd
Much poor, if not by thee preserv'd,
Whose prayers have made thy table bless'd
With plenty, far above the rest.
The season hardly did afford
Coarse cates[1] unto thy neighbours' board,
Yet thou hadst dainties, as the sky
Had only been thy volary;
Or else the birds, fearing the snow
Might to another Deluge grow,
The pheasant, partridge, and the lark
Flew to thy house, as to the Ark.
The willing ox of himself came
Home to the slaughter, with the lamb,
And every beast did thither bring
Himself, to be an offering.
The scaly herd more pleasure took,
Bath'd in thy dish, than in the brook;
Water, earth, air, did all conspire
To pay their tributes to thy fire,
Whose cherishing flames themselves divide
Through every room, where they deride
The night and cold abroad; whilst they,
Like suns within, keep endless day.
Those cheerful beams send forth their light
To all that wander in the night,
And seem to beckon from aloof
The weary pilgrim to thy roof;
Where if, refresh'd, he will away,
He's fairly welcome; or if stay,
Far more; which he shall hearty find
Both from the master and the hind:
The stranger's welcome each man there
Stamp'd on his cheerful brow doth wear.
Nor doth this welcome or his cheer
Grow less 'cause he stays longer here:
There's none observes, much less repines,

---

[1]*cates*: delicacies.

How often this man sups or dines.
Thou hast no porter at the door
T' examine or keep back the poor;
Nor locks nor bolts: thy gates have bin
Made only to let strangers in;
Untaught to shut, they do not fear
To stand wide open all the year,
Careless who enters, for they know
Thou never didst deserve a foe:
And as for thieves, thy bounty's such,
They cannot steal, thou giv'st so much.

To a Lady That Desired I Would Love Her

Now you have freely given me leave to love,
                     What will you do?
Shall I your mirth or passion move
                     When I begin to woo?
Will you torment, or scorn, or love me too?

Each petty beauty can disdain, and I,
                     Spite of your hate,
Without your leave can see, and die.
                     Dispense a nobler fate!
'Tis easy to destroy: you may create.

Then give me leave to love, and love me too:
                     Not with design
To raise, as Love's curs'd rebels do,
                     When puling poets whine,
Fame to their beauty from their blubb'red eyne.[1]

Grief is a puddle, and reflects not clear
                     Your beauty's rays;
Joys are pure streams; your eyes appear
                     Sullen in sadder lays:
In cheerful numbers they shine bright with praise,

Which shall not mention, to express you fair,
                     Wounds, flames, and darts,
Storms in your brow, nets in your hair,
                     Suborning all your parts,
Or to betray or torture captive hearts.

---

[1]*eyne*: eyes.

I'll make your eyes like morning suns appear,
     As mild and fair;
Your brow as crystal smooth and clear;
      And your dishevell'd hair
Shall flow like a calm region of the air.

Rich Nature's store, which is the poet's treasure,
     I'll spend to dress
Your beauties, if your mine of pleasure
      In equal thankfulness
You but unlock, so we each other bless.

To Ben Jonson

*Upon occasion of his Ode of Defiance[1] annex'd to his Play of
The New Inn*

'Tis true (dear Ben) thy just chastising hand
Hath fixt upon the sotted age a brand
To their swollen pride, and empty scribbling due,
It can nor judge, nor write, and yet 'tis true
Thy comic muse from the exalted line
Touch'd by thy Alchemist, doth since decline
From that her zenith, and foretells a red
And blushing evening, when she goes to bed,
Yet such, as shall out-shine the glimmering light
With which all stars shall guild the following night.
Nor think it much (since all thy eaglets may
Endure the sunny trial)[2] if we say
This hath the stronger wing, or that doth shine
Trick'd up in fairer plumes, since all are thine;
Who hath his flock of cackling geese compar'd
With thy tun'd choir of swans? or else who dar'd
To call thy births deformed? but if thou bind
By city-custom,[3] or by gavell-kind,[4]

---

[1]*Ode of Defiance*: Jonson's "Come leave the loathed stage," which he wrote in
 response to the hooting of his play "The New Inn."
[2]*sunny trial*: the idea being that a mother eagle tests her offspring by forcing them
 to look directly into the sun.
[3]*city-custom*: an institution by which the property of a deceased London citizen
 was equally divided between the widow, executors and children.
[4]*gavell-kind*: an institution in Kent by which land was equally divided among the
 sons of the deceased.

In equal shares thy love on all thy race,
We may distinguish of their sex, and place;
Though one hand form them, & though one brain strike
Souls into all, they are not all alike.
Why should the follies then of this dull age
Draw from thy pen such an immodest rage
As seems to blast thy (else-immortal) bays,
When thine own tongue proclaims thy itch of praise?
Such thirst will argue drouth. No, let be hurl'd
Upon thy works, by the detracting world,
What malice can suggest; let the rout[1] say,
The running sands, that (ere thou make a play)
Count the slow minutes, might a Goodwin[2] frame
To swallow when th' hast done thy ship-wrack'd name.
Let them the dear expense of oil upbraid
Suck'd by thy watchful lamp, that hath betray'd
To theft the blood of martyr'd authors, spilt
Into thy ink, whilst thou growest pale with guilt.
Repine not at the taper's thrifty waste,
That sleeks thy terser poems, nor is haste
Praise, but excuse; and if thou overcome
A knotty writer, bring the booty home;
Nor think it theft, if the rich spoils so torn
From conquered authors, be as trophies worn.
Let others glut on the extorted praise
Of vulgar breath, trust thou to after days:
Thy labour'd works shall live, when Time devours
Th' abortive off-spring of their hasty hours.
Thou art not of their rank, the quarrel lies
Within thine own verge, then let this suffice,
The wiser world doth greater thee confess
Than all men else, than thyself only less.

---

[1]*rout*: mob.
[2]*Goodwin*: the Goodwin Sands, a line of shoals in the Strait of Dover on which
  many ships were wrecked.

SIR JOHN SUCKLING

HAVING INHERITED a large estate, and possessing good looks and a lively spirit, Sir John Suckling (1609–1642) was an admired presence at court from the age of eighteen. In the summer of 1631 he was part of a military effort backing Gustavus II Adolphus of Sweden in his Bavarian campaign (in which Gustavus himself was killed on the battlefield). On his return to London, Suckling is said to have entered into gambling and drinking with prodigal enthusiasm. During this period he wrote not only verse but several masques which were performed at court (Charles was very fond of masques, even participating in a few; this is said to have disgusted Cromwell, who, as Lord Protector, would outlaw the theater). The most famous of Suckling's masques, *Aglaura*, fared badly with the critics, but, like his other dramatic efforts, yielded some fine lyrics, including "Why so pale and wan, fond lover?"

In 1639 (during the First Bishop's War) Suckling marched with his own contingent of a hundred troops in the Scottish Campaign, accompanying Charles in his advance to the border (and subsequently in his retreat from it). Though Suckling was ridiculed by London wits for outfitting his militia with gorgeous scarlet coats and ostrich-plumed hats, his performance in the field raised him in the estimation of his king. Suckling's further adventures are enough to fill a book: amorous intrigues in Paris necessitating flight from the country; near-execution in Spain on false charges of conspiring to murder Philip IV; and, according to some reports, torture at the hands of the Inquisition. He is then said to have married and settled in Holland. Reduced in means and crushed by debt, Suckling committed suicide in 1642.

Most of Suckling's work first appeared in a posthumous volume entitled *Fragmenta Aurea: A Collection of All the Incomparable Peeces written by Sir John Suckling; and Published by a Friend to Perpetuate His Memory.* Suckling's verse, of course, smacks of the court: it is witty, decorous, sometimes naughty; all requisites for the courtier poet. But these qualities alone would not have sufficed to "perpetuate his memory." It should be remembered that the court swarmed with now-forgotten versifiers. Suckling had his own voice, a deft conversational ease mixed at times with a certain hauteur or swagger, which qualities were not incompatible with his high birth and military occupation. In fact, though this is to some extent true of all the Cavaliers, Suckling especially favored military imagery and subject matter, and in poems like " 'Tis now, since I sate down before" and "A Soldier," he cultivates the persona of the Cavalier perfectly. Though his oeuvre is comparatively small, Suckling is an exemplary lyric poet, as well as one of the most vivid personalities of his age.

Song

Why so pale and wan, fond lover?
   Prithee, why so pale?
Will, when looking well can't move her,
    Looking ill prevail?
    Prithee, why so pale?

Why so dull and mute, young sinner?
   Prithee, why so mute?
Will, when speaking well can't win her,
    Saying nothing do 't?
    Prithee, why so mute?

Quit, quit, for shame; this will not move,
   This cannot take her;
If of herself she will not love,
    Nothing can make her:
    The devil take her!

Sonnet I

Dost see how unregarded now
   That piece of beauty passes?
There was a time when I did vow
    To that alone;
    But mark the fate of faces;
The red and white works now no more on me,
Than if it could not charm, or I not see.

And yet the face continues good,
   And I have still desires,
Am still the selfsame flesh and blood,
    As apt to melt,
    And suffer from those fires;
Oh, some kind power unriddle where it lies,
Whether my heart be faulty, or her eyes.

She every day her man does kill,
   And I as often die;
Neither her power, then, nor my will
    Can question'd be,

What is the mystery?
Sure beauty's empires, like to greater states,
Have certain periods set, and hidden fates.

Sonnet II

Of thee (kind boy) I ask no red and white,
                To make up my delight;
                No odd becoming graces,
Black eyes, or little know-not-whats, in faces;
Make me but mad enough, give me good store
Of love for her I court:
                I ask no more,
'Tis love in love that makes the sport.

There's no such thing as that we beauty call,
                It is mere cozenage all;
                For though some long ago
Lik'd certain colours mingled so and so,
That doth not tie me now from choosing new:
If I a fancy take
                To black and blue,
That fancy doth it beauty make.

'Tis not the meat, but 'tis the appetite
                Makes eating a delight,
                And if I like one dish
More than another, that a pheasant is;
What in our watches, that in us is found;
So to the height and nick
                We up be wound,
No matter by what hand or trick.

Sonnet III

O for some honest lover's ghost,
                Some kind unbodied post
                Sent from the shades below!
                I strangely long to know
Whether the nobler chaplets wear,

Those that their mistress' scorn did bear,
             Or those that were us'd kindly.

For whatsoe'er they tell us here
             To make those sufferings dear,
             'Twill there I fear be found,
             That to the being crown'd
T' have lov'd alone will not suffice,
Unless we also have been wise,
             And have our loves enjoy'd.

What posture can we think him in,
             That here unlov'd agen
             Departs, and 's thither gone,
             Where each sits by his own?
Or how can that Elysium be,
Where I my mistress still must see
             Circled in others' arms?

For there the judges all are just,
             And Sophonisba[1] must
             Be his whom she held dear,
             Not his who lov'd her here:
The sweet Philoclea, since she di'd,
Lies by her Pirocles his side,
             Not by Amphialus.[2]

Some bays, perchance, or myrtle bough,
             For difference crowns the brow
             Of those kind souls that were
             The noble martyrs here;
And if that be the only odds
(As who can tell?), ye kinder gods,
             Give me the woman here.

---

[1]*Sophonisba*: (d. ca. 204 B.C.) a Carthaginian woman who was betrothed to the
  Numidian Prince Masinissa, but was married, for political reasons, to Syphax, a
  rival prince. When Masinissa defeated Syphax, he and Sophonisba were re-
  united and married. When they were subsequently separated again, in the
  Punic Wars, she committed suicide by drinking poison which her husband had
  sent her, to prevent her falling into the hands of the Romans.

[2]*Philoclea . . . Amphialus*: a love triangle, similar to that outlined in the above
  note, from Sir Philip Sidney's *Arcadia* (1590).

Against Fruition

Stay here, fond youth, and ask no more; be wise:
Knowing too much long since lost paradise.
The virtuous joys thou hast, thou wouldst should still
Last in their pride; and wouldst not take it ill,
If rudely from sweet dreams (and for a toy)
Thou wert wak'd? he wakes himself, that does enjoy.

Fruition adds no new wealth, but destroys,
And while it pleaseth much the palate, cloys;
Who thinks he shall be happier for that,
As reasonably might hope he might grow fat
By eating to a surfeit; this once past,
What relishes? even kisses lose their taste.

Urge not 'tis necessary: alas! we know
The homeliest thing which mankind does is so;
The world is of a vast extent, we see,
And must be peopled; children there must be;
So must bread too; but since they are enough
Born to the drudgery, what need we plough?

Women enjoy'd (whate'er before th' have been)
Are like romances read, or sights once seen;
Fruition's dull, and spoils the play much more
Than if one read or knew the plot before;
'Tis expectation makes a blessing dear,
Heaven were not heaven, if we knew what it were.

And as in prospects we are there pleas'd most,
Where something keeps the eye from being lost,
And leaves us room to guess; so here restraint
Holds up delight, that with excess would faint.
They who know all the wealth they have are poor;
He's only rich that cannot tell his store.

Woman's Constancy

There never yet was woman made,
        Nor shall, but to be curs'd;
And oh, that I, fond I, should first,
        Of any lover,
This truth at my own charge to other fools discover!

You that have promis'd to yourselves
> Propriety in love,
Know, women's hearts like straw do move;
> And what we call
Their sympathy, is but love to jet[1] in general.

All mankind are alike to them;
> And though we iron find
That never with a loadstone join'd,
> 'Tis not the iron's fault,
It is because the loadstone yet was never brought.

If, where a gentle bee hath fall'n,
> And labour'd to his power,
A new succeeds not to that flower,
> But passes by,
'Tis to be thought, the gallant elsewhere loads his thigh.

For still the flowers ready stand:
> One buzzes round about,
One lights, and tastes, gets in, gets out;
> All all ways use them,
Till all their sweets are gone, and all again refuse them.

Song

No, no, fair heretic, it needs must be
> But an ill love in me,
> And worse for thee:
For were it in my power
To love thee now this hour
> More than I did the last,
'Twould then so fall
> I might not love at all:
Love that can flow, and can admit increase,
Admits as well an ebb, and may grow less.

True love is still the same: the torrid zones,
> And those more frigid ones,
> It must not know;

---

[1] *jet*: The Oxford English Dictionary cites this line of Suckling's in its definition of "jet" as a type of coal that "has the power of attracting light bodies when rubbed."

For love grown cold or hot
Is lust or friendship, not
      The thing we have,
For that's a flame would die,
      Held down or up too high.
Then think I love more than I can express,
And would love more, could I but love thee less.

"Love, Reason, Hate, did once bespeak"

Love, Reason, Hate, did once bespeak
Three mates to play at barley-break:[1]
Love Folly took; and Reason, Fancy;
And Hate consorts with Pride; so dance they:
Love coupled last, and so it fell,
That Love and Folly were in hell.

They break, and Love would Reason meet,
But Hate was nimbler on her feet;
Fancy looks for Pride, and thither
Hies, and they two hug together:
Yet this new coupling still doth tell
That Love and Folly were in hell.

The rest do break again, and Pride
Hath now got Reason on her side;
Hate and Fancy meet, and stand
Untouch'd by Love in Folly's hand;
Folly was dull, but Love ran well:
So Love and Folly were in hell.

Song

I prithee spare me, gentle boy,
Press me no more for that slight toy,
That foolish trifle of an heart;
I swear it will not do its part,
Though thou dost thine, employ'st thy power and art.

---

[1]*barley-break*: an ancient rural game in which one couple is placed in a middle
    space, called *hell*, and then tries to catch the others, who break or scatter when
    chased.

For through long custom it has known
The little secrets, and is grown
Sullen and wise, will have its will,
And, like old hawks, pursues that still
That makes least sport, flies only where 't can kill.

Some youth that has not made his story,
Will think, perchance, the pain's the glory,
And mannerly sit out love's feast:
I shall be carving of the best,
Rudely call for the last course 'fore the rest.

And, oh, when once that course is past,
How short a time the feast doth last!
Men rise away, and scarce say grace,
Or civilly once thank the face
That did invite, but seek another place.

Upon My Lady Carlile's Walking in Hampton Court Garden

Dialogue

T.C.   J.S.[1]

Tom. Didst thou not find the place inspir'd,
And flowers, as if they had desir'd
No other sun, start from their beds,
And for a sight steal out their heads?
Heard'st thou not music when she talk'd?
And didst not find that as she walk'd
She threw rare perfumes all about,
Such as bean-blossoms newly out,
Or chafed spices give? ——

J. S. I must confess those perfumes (Tom)
I did not smell; nor found that from
Her passing by aught sprung up new:
The flow'rs had all their birth from you;
For I pass'd o'er the selfsame walk,
And did not find one single stalk
Of any thing that was to bring
This unknown after-after-Spring.

---

[1]The speakers are Thomas Carew and John Suckling.

Tom.   Dull and insensible, couldst see
    A thing so near a deity
    Move up and down, and feel no change?

J. S.   None and so great were alike strange.
    I had my thoughts, but not your way;
    All are not born, sir, to the bay;
    Alas! Tom, I am flesh and blood,
    And was consulting how I could
    In spite of masks and hoods descry
    The parts denied unto the eye:
    I was undoing all she wore;
    And had she walk'd but one turn more,
    Eve in her first state had not been
    More naked, or more plainly seen.

Tom.   'Twas well for thee she left the place;
    There is great danger in that face;
    But hadst thou view'd her leg and thigh,
    And upon that discovery
    Search'd after parts that are more dear
    (As fancy seldom stops so near),
    No time or age had ever seen
    So lost a thing as thou hadst been.

Against Absence

My whining lover, what needs all
These vows of life monastical,
Despairs, retirements, jealousies,
And subtle sealing up of eyes?
Come, come, be wise; return again;
A finger burnt's as great a pain:
And the same physic, selfsame art
Cures that, would cure a flaming heart,
Wouldst thou, whilst yet the fire is in,
But hold it to the fire again.
If you, dear sir, the plague have got,
What matter is 't whether or not
They let you in the same house lie,
Or carry you abroad to die?
He whom the plague or love once takes,

Every room a pest-house makes.
Absence were good if 'twere but sense
That only holds th' intelligence.
Pure love alone no hurt would do;
But love is love and magic too:
Brings a mistress a thousand miles,
And the sleight of looks beguiles,
Makes her entertain thee there,
And the same time your rival here;
And (oh the devil!) that she should
Say finer things now than she would;
So nobly fancy doth supply
What the dull sense lets fall and die.
Beauty, like man's old enemy, 's known
To tempt him most when he's alone:
The air of some wild o'ergrown wood
Or pathless grove is the boy's food.
Return then back, and feed thine eye,
Feed all thy senses, and feast high:
Spare diet is the cause love lasts,
For surfeits sooner kill than fasts.

A *Supplement of an Imperfect Copy of Verses of Mr. Will. Shakespeare's, by the Author*

One of her hands one of her cheeks lay under,
   Cozening the pillow of a lawful kiss,
Which therefore swell'd, and seem'd to part asunder,
   As angry to be robb'd of such a bliss:
      The one look'd pale, and for revenge did long,
      While t' other blush'd, 'cause it had done the wrong.

Out of the bed the other fair hand was
   On a green satin quilt, whose perfect white
Look'd like a daisy in a field of grass,
   And show'd like unmelt snow unto the sight:
      There lay this pretty perdue,[1] safe to keep
      The rest o' th' body that lay fast asleep.

---

[1]*perdue*: a soldier sent on a perilous mission.

Her eyes (and therefore it was night), close laid,
   Strove to imprison beauty till the morn;
But yet the doors were of such fine stuff made,
    That it broke through, and show'd itself in scorn,
      Throwing a kind of light about the place,
      Which turn'd to smiles still as 't came near her face.

Her beams, which some dull men call'd hair, divided,
   Part with her cheeks, part with her lips did sport;
But these, as rude, her breath put by still; some
   Wiselier downwards sought, but falling short,
     Curl'd back in rings, and seem'd to turn agen
     To bite the part so unkindly held them in.

" *'Tis now, since I sate down before*"[1]

'Tis now, since I sate down before
   That foolish fort, a heart,
(Time strangely spent) a year and more,
   And still I did my part:

Made my approaches, from her hand
   Unto her lip did rise,
And did already understand
   The language of her eyes;

Proceeded on with no less art—
   My tongue was engineer:
I thought to undermine the heart
   By whispering in the ear.

When this did nothing, I brought down
   Great cannon-oaths, and shot
A thousand thousand to the town;
   And still it yielded not.

I then resolv'd to starve the place
   By cutting off all kisses,
Praising and gazing on her face,
   And all such little blisses.

---

[1]*sit down before*: archaic military term for "lay siege to."

To draw her out, and from her strength,
    I drew all batteries in;
And brought myself to lie at length,
    As if no siege had been.

When I had done what man could do,
    And thought the place mine own,
The enemy lay quiet too,
    And smil'd at all was done.

I sent to know from whence and where
    These hopes and this relief:
A spy inform'd, Honour was there,
    And did command in chief.

March, march, quoth I, the word straight give,
    Let's lose no time, but leave her;
That giant upon air will live,
    And hold it out for ever.

To such a place our camp remove
    As will no siege abide;
I hate a fool that starves her love,
    Only to feed her pride.

Loving and Beloved

There never yet was honest man
    That ever drove the trade of love;
It is impossible, nor can
    Integrity our ends promove;[1]
For kings and lovers are alike in this,
That their chief art in reign dissembling is.

Here we are lov'd, and there we love;
    Good nature now and passion strive
Which of the two should be above,
    And laws unto the other give.
So we false fire with art sometimes discover,
And the true fire with the same art do cover.

---

[1]*promove*: promote.

What rack can fancy find so high?
　　Here we must court, and here engage,
Though in the other place we die.
　　Oh, 'tis torture all, and cozenage!
And which the harder is I cannot tell,
To hide true love, or make false love look well.

Since it is thus, God of Desire,
　　Give me my honesty again,
And take thy brands back, and thy fire;
　　I am weary of the state I'm in:
Since (if the very best should now befall)
Love's triumph must be Honour's funeral.

"My dearest rival, lest our love"

My dearest rival, lest our love
Should with eccentric motion move,
Before it learn to go astray,
We'll teach and set it in a way,
And such directions give unto 't,
That it shall never wander foot.
Know first then, we will serve as true
For one poor smile, as we would do,
If we had what our higher flame
Or our vainer wish could frame.
Impossible shall be our hope;
And love shall only have his scope
To join with fancy now and then,
And think what reason would condemn:
And on these grounds we'll love as true,
As if they were most sure t' ensue:
And chastely for these things we'll stay,
As if to-morrow were the day.
Meantime we two will teach our hearts
In love's burdens bear their parts:
Thou first shall sigh, and say she's fair;
And I'll still answer, past compare.
Thou shalt set out each part o' th' face,
While I extol each little grace;
Thou shalt be ravish'd at her wit,
And I, that she so governs it;

Thou shalt like well that hand, that eye,
That lip, that look, that majesty,
And in good language them adore;
While I want words and do it more.
Yea, we will sit and sigh a while,
And with soft thoughts some time beguile;
But straight again break out, and praise
All we had done before, new-ways.
Thus will we do till paler death
Come with a warrant for our breath,
And then, whose fate shall be to die
First of us two, by legacy
Shall all his store bequeath, and give
His love to him that shall survive;
For no one stock can ever serve
To love so much as she'll deserve.

Farewell to Love

Well-shadow'd landskip,[1] fare ye well:
How I have lov'd you none can tell,
    At least, so well
  As he that now hates more
  Than e'er he lov'd before.

But my dear nothings, take your leave:
No longer must you me deceive,
    Since I perceive
  All the deceit, and know
  Whence the mistake did grow.

As he whose quicker eye doth trace
A false star shot to a mark'd place,
    Does run apace,
  And thinking it to catch,
  A jelly up does snatch:

So our dull souls, tasting delight
Far off, by sense and appetite,
    Think that is right
  And real good; when yet
  'Tis but the counterfeit.

---

[1] *landskip*: landscape.

Oh, how I glory now, that I
Have made this new discovery!
   Each wanton eye
  Inflam'd before: no more
  Will I increase that score.

If I gaze now, 'tis but to see
What manner of death's-head 'twill be,
   When it is free
  From that fresh upper skin,
  The gazer's joy and sin.

The gum and glist'ning which with art
And studied method in each part
   Hangs down the hair, 't
  Looks (just) as if that day
  Snails there had crawl'd the hay.

The locks that curl'd o'er each ear be,
Hang like two master-worms to me,
   That (as we see)
  Have tasted to the rest
  Two holes, where they like 't best.

A quick corse, methinks, I spy
In ev'ry woman; and mine eye,
   At passing by,
  Checks, and is troubled, just
  As if it rose from dust.

They mortify, not heighten me;
These of my sins the glasses be;
   And here I see
  How I have lov'd before.
  And so I love no more.

Love and Debt Alike Troublesome

  This one request I make to him that sits the clouds above
  That I were freely out of debt, as I am out of love:
Then for to dance, to drink and sing, I should be very willing
I should not owe one lass a kiss, nor ne'r a knave a shilling.
'Tis only being in Love and Debt, that breaks us of our rest;
And he that is quite out of both, of all the world is bless'd:

He sees the golden age wherein all things were free and common;
He eats, he drinks, he takes his rest, he fears no man nor woman.
Though Croesus compassed great wealth, yet he still craved more,
He was as needy a beggar still, as goes from door to door.
Though Ovid were a merry man, Love ever kept him sad;
He was as far from happiness, as one that is stark mad.
Our Merchant he in goods is rich, and full of gold and treasure;
But when he thinks upon his Debts, that thought destroys his
    pleasure.
Our Courtier thinks that he's preferr'd, whom every man envies;
When Love so rumbles in his pate, no sleep comes in his eyes.
Our Gallant's case is worst of all, he lies so just betwixt them;
For he's in Love, and he's in Debt, and knows not which most vex
    him.
But he that can eat beef, and feed on bread which is so brown
May satisfy his appetite, and owe no man a crown:
And he that is content with lasses clothed in plain woollen,
May cool his heat in every place, he need not to be sullen,
Nor sigh for love of lady fair; for this each wise man knows,
As good stuff under flannel lies, as under silken clothes.

Out upon It

Out upon it, I have lov'd
    Three whole days together;
And am like to love three more,
    If it prove fair weather.

Time shall moult away his wings,
    Ere he shall discover
In the whole wide world again
    Such a constant lover.

But the spite on 't is, no praise
    Is due at all to me:
Love with me had made no stays,
    Had it any been but she.

Had it any been but she,
    And that very face,
There had been at least ere this
    A dozen dozen in her place.

A Soldier

I am a man of war and might,
And know thus much, that I can fight,
Whether I am i' th' wrong or right,
                                    Devoutly.

No woman under heaven I fear,
New oaths I can exactly swear,
And forty healths my brain will bear
                                    Most stoutly.

I cannot speak, but I can do
As much as any of our crew;
And if you doubt it, some of you
                                    May prove me.

I dare be bold thus much to say:
If that my bullets do but play,
You would be hurt so night and day,
                                    Yet love me.

RICHARD LOVELACE

RICHARD LOVELACE (1618–1658) was a scion of the old Kentish family which distinguished itself in the court of Elizabeth I. Like Suckling, Lovelace saw military action in the Royalist effort. His most famous lines, however, are not of the field, but of the dungeon: "Stone walls do not a prison make, / Nor iron bars a cage" ("To Althea, from Prison").

Lovelace was incarcerated twice in his life. The first occasion resulted from his presentation of a Royalist petition to Parliament, thereby aligning himself with such notorious Royalist upstarts as Sir Edmund Dering (whose own such petition had already landed him in jail). Lovelace was imprisoned in Westminster Gatehouse from April 30 to June 21, 1642. On his release, he immediately began mustering troops, which he employed on the field with some success, following Charles to Oxford. When Charles was captured there in 1646 (effectively ending his career), Lovelace went to France, raised a militia and fought for the French king, then at war with Spain. Lovelace left the field when he was wounded at the battle of Dunkirk. On his return to (Cromwell's) England, in 1648, he was promptly jailed, and then discharged in April 1649. He died — in poverty, it is thought — in 1658, and was buried at St. Bride's (one of the churches destroyed in the Great Fire of 1666).

Lovelace's songs to Lucasta and Althea are some of the finest lyrics of the period, notable for their wit, soldierly nobility and high level of craftsmanship. "Song: To Lucasta, Going to the Wars" is one of the undisputed masterpieces of English poetry. And pieces such as "Gratiana Dancing and Singing," "Elinda's Glove" and "Lucasta Laughing," brilliant *carpe diem* poems, record in their own way the feeling, among those loyal to the king, that upheaval was looming (or had indeed arrived), and that moments of happiness were to be savored and preserved. The longer poem "The Lady A. L.: My Asylum in a Great Extremity," probably addressed to a cousin, Anne Lovelace, manages, among other things, an ingenious synthesis of the experience of a deposed king and that of an ordinary person broken by hard fate. It is a particularly good example of that propensity in the Cavaliers to shift easily from the brief, witty lyric to the carefully crafted, moving soliloquy. Another of Lovelace's finest pieces is the lovely, lilting poem "The Grasshopper," in which the poet takes a uniquely philosophical view of the pressing "Winter" of Cromwell's England; the poem also displays the poet's subtle sense of humor and eye for natural imagery. Like Suckling, Lovelace produced only a small body of work.

Song

To Lucasta, Going Beyond the Seas

If to be absent were to be
        Away from thee;
        Or that when I am gone
        You or I were alone;
Then, my Lucasta, might I crave
Pity from blust'ring wind, or swallowing wave.

But I'll not sigh one blast or gale
        To swell my sail,
        Or pay a tear to swage[1]
        The foaming blue god's rage;[2]
For whether he will let me pass
Or no, I'm still as happy as I was.

Though seas and land betwixt us both,
        Our faith and troth,
        Like separated souls,
        All time and space controls:
Above the highest sphere we meet
Unseen, unknown, and greet as angels greet.

So then we do anticipate
        Our after-fate,
        And are alive i' th' skies,
        If thus our lips and eyes
Can speak like spirits unconfin'd
In heav'n, their earthy bodies left behind.

---

[1]*swage*: assuage.
[2]*blue god*: Poseidon, god of the sea.

Song

To Lucasta, Going to the Wars

Tell me not (sweet) I am unkind,
　That from the nunnery
Of thy chaste breast and quiet mind,
　To war and arms I fly.

True; a new mistress now I chase,
　The first foe in the field;
And with a stronger faith embrace
　A sword, a horse, a shield.

Yet this inconstancy is such
　As you too shall adore;
I could not love thee (dear) so much,
　Lov'd I not Honour more.

Song

To Amarantha, that She Would Dishevel Her Hair

　Amarantha sweet and fair,
Ah braid no more that shining hair!
　As my curious hand or eye,
Hovering round thee let it fly.

　Let it fly as unconfin'd
As its calm ravisher, the wind,
　Who hath left his darling, th' East,
To wanton o'er that spicy nest.

　Ev'ry tress must be confess'd
But neatly tangled at the best;
　Like a clew of golden thread
Most excellently ravelled.

　Do not then wind up that light
In ribbands, and o'ercloud in night;
　Like the sun in 's early ray,
But shake your head and scatter day.

See, 'tis broke! Within this grove,
The bower and the walks of love,
   Weary lie we down and rest,
And fan each other's panting breast.

Here we'll strip and cool our fire
In cream below, in milk-baths higher;
   And when all wells are drawn dry,
I'll drink a tear out of thine eye,

Which our very joys shall leave,
That sorrows thus we can deceive;
   Or our very sorrows weep,
That joys so ripe so little keep.

Sonnet

Depose your finger of that ring,
   And crown mine with 't awhile.
Now I restore 't—Pray does it bring
   Back with it more of soil?
Or shines it not as innocent,
As honest, as before 'twas lent?

So then enrich me with that treasure
   Will but increase your store,
And please me, fair one, with that pleasure
   Must please you still the more:
Not to save others is a curse
The blackest, when y' are ne'er the worse.

Ode

To Lucasta. The Rose

Sweet, serene, sky-like flower,
Haste to adorn her bower:
   From thy long cloudy bed
   Shoot forth thy damask head.

New-startled blush of Flora!
The grief of pale Aurora,[1]
   Who will contest no more,
   Haste, haste, to strow her floor.

Vermilion ball that's given
From lip to lip in heaven;
   Love's couch's coverled,[2]
   Haste, haste, to make her bed.

Dear offspring of pleas'd Venus
And jolly plump Silenus,[3]
   Haste, haste, to deck the hair
   Of th' only sweetly fair.

See! rosy is her bower,
Her floor is all this flower,
   Her bed a rosy nest
   By a bed of roses press'd.

But early as she dresses,
Why fly you her bright tresses?
   Ah! I have found I fear:
   Because her cheeks are near.

Gratiana Dancing and Singing

See! with what constant motion,
Even and glorious as the sun,
   Gratiana steers that noble frame.
Soft as her breast, sweet as her voice
That gave each winding law and poise,
   And swifter than the wings of Fame,

She beat the happy pavëment
By such a star made firmament,
   Which now no more the roof envies,
But swells up high with Atlas ev'n,

---

[1]*Flora, Aurora*: goddesses of flowers and dawn, respectively.
[2]*coverled*: coverlet.
[3]*Silenus*: in classical mythology the son of Pan, usually depicted smiling drunk-
   enly.

Bearing the brighter, nobler heav'n,
   And, in her, all the deities.

Each step trod out a lover's thought
And the ambitious hopes he brought,
   Chain'd to her brave feet with such arts,
Such sweet command and gentle awe,
As when she ceas'd, we sighing saw
   The floor lay pav'd with broken hearts.

So did she move; so did she sing
Like the harmonious spheres that bring
   Unto their rounds their music's aid;
Which she performed such a way,
As all th' enamour'd world will say
   The Graces danced, and Apollo play'd.

Song

The Scrutiny

Why should you swear I am forsworn,
   Since thine I vow'd to be?
Lady, it is already morn,
   And 'twas last night I swore to thee
That fond impossibility.

Have I not lov'd thee much and long,
   A tedious twelve hours' space?
I must all other beauties wrong,
   And rob thee of a new embrace,
Could I still dote upon thy face.

Not but all joy in thy brown hair
   By others may be found;
But I must search the black and fair,
   Like skilful mineralists that sound
For treasure in unplough'd-up ground.

Then if, when I have lov'd my round,
   Thou prov'st the pleasant she,
With spoils of meaner beauties crown'd,
   I laden will return to thee,
Ev'n sated with variety.

The Grasshopper[1]

To My Noble Friend Mr. Charles Cotton.[2] *Ode*

O thou that swing'st upon the waving hair
   Of some well-filled oaten beard,
Drunk ev'ry night with a delicious tear
   Dropt thee from heav'n, where now th' art rear'd.

The joys of earth and air are thine entire,
   That with thy feet and wings dost hop and fly;
And when thy poppy works thou dost retire
   To thy carv'd acorn-bed to lie.

Up with the day, the sun thou welcom'st then,
   Sport'st in the gilt-plats[3] of his beams,
And all these merry days mak'st merry men,
   Thyself, and melancholy streams.

But ah the sickle! golden ears are cropp'd
   Ceres and Bacchus bid good night;
Sharp frosty fingers all your flow'rs have topp'd
   And what scythes spar'd, winds shave off quite.

Poor verdant fool, and now green ice! thy joys,
   Large and as lasting as thy perch of grass,
Bid us lay in 'gainst winter rain, and poise
   Their floods with an o'erflowing glass.

Thou best of men and friends! we will create
   A genuine Summer in each other's breast;
And spite of this cold Time and frozen Fate,
   Thaw us a warm seat to our rest.

Our sacred hearths shall burn eternally
   As vestal flames; the North-wind, he
Shall strike his frost-stretch'd wings, dissolve, and fly
   This Etna in epitome.

---

[1]*The Grasshopper*: cf. the "grasshopper" lyric of the Greek poet Anacreon (572?–?488 B.C.), which was translated by Lovelace's contemporary, Abraham Cowley (1618–1667).
[2]*Charles Cotton*: (d. 1658) cf. note to Herrick's poem to Cotton (page 23).
[3]*gilt-plats*: gilded plates, i.e. the sun's rays.

Dropping December shall come weeping in,
 Bewail th' usurping of his reign;
But when in show'rs of old Greek we begin,
 Shall cry he hath his crown again!

Night as clear Hesper[1] shall our tapers whip
 From the light casements where we play,
And the dark hag from her black mantle strip,
 And stick there everlasting day.

Thus richer than untempted kings are we,
 That asking nothing, nothing need:
Though lord of all what seas embrace, yet he
 That wants himself, is poor indeed.

Dialogue

Lucasta. Alexis

Lucasta. Tell me, Alexis, what this parting is,
    That so like dying is, but is not it.
 Alexis. It is a swounding for a while from bliss,
    Till kind "How do you?" calls us from the fit.
    If then the spirits only stray, let mine
    Fly to thy bosom. *Lucasta.* And my soul to thine.

Chorus

    Thus in our native seat we gladly give
    Our right for one where we can better live.

Lucasta. But ah this ling'ring, murd'ring farewell!
    Death quickly wounds, and wounding cures the ill.
 Alexis. It is the glory of a valiant lover
    Still to be dying, still for to recover.

Chorus

    Soldiers suspected of their courage go,
    That ensigns and their breasts untorn show:
    Love near his standard when his host he sets,
    Creates alone fresh-bleeding bannerets.

---

[1]*Hesper*: the planet Venus.

Alexis.   But part we when thy figure I retain
            Still in my heart, still strongly in mine eye?
Lucasta. Shadows no longer than the sun remain,
            But when his beams, that made 'em, fly, they fly.

Chorus

Vain dreams of love! that only so much bliss
Allow us, as to know our wretchedness;
And deal a larger measure in our pain,
By showing joy, then hiding it again.

Alexis.   No, whilst light reigns, Lucasta still rules here,
            And all the night shines wholly in this sphere.
Lucasta. I know no morn but my Alexis' ray,
            To my dark thoughts the breaking of the day.

Chorus

Alexis.   So in each other if the pitying sun
            Thus keep us fix'd, ne'er may his course be run!
Lucasta. And oh! if night us undivided make,
            Let us sleep still, and sleeping, never wake!

The Close

Cruel adieus may well adjourn awhile
The sessions of a look, a kiss, or smile,
And leave behind an angry grieving blush;
But time nor fate can part us joined thus.

To Elinda

That Lately I Have Not Written

If in me anger, or disdain
In you, or both, made me refrain
From th' noble intercourse of verse,
That only virtuous thoughts rehearse;
   Then, chaste Elinda, might you fear
   The sacred vows that I did swear.

But if alone some pious thought
Me to an inward sadness brought;
Thinking to breathe your soul too well,

My tongue was charmed with that spell,
   And left it (since there was no room
     To voice your worth enough) strook dumb.

To Lucasta

From Prison. An Epode[1]

Long in thy shackles, liberty
I ask, not from these walls but thee
(Left for awhile another's bride),
To fancy all the world beside.

Yet ere I do begin to love,
See! how I all my objects prove;
Then my free soul to that confine
'Twere possible I might call mine.

First I would be in love with Peace,
And her rich swelling breasts' increase;
But how, alas! how may that be,
Despising earth, she will love me?

Fain would I be in love with War,
As my dear just avenging star;
But War is lov'd so ev'rywhere,
Ev'n he disdains a lodging here.

Thee and thy wounds I would bemoan,
Fair thorough-shot Religion;
But he lives only that kills thee,
And whoso binds thy hands is free.

I would love a Parliament
As a main prop from heav'n sent;
But ah! who's he that would be wedded
To th' fairest body that's beheaded?[2]

---

[1]*Epode*: Greek lyric stanza forming the third part of a classic ode (following
   the *strophe* and *antistrophe*). It was also developed as a satirical form by
   Horace.
[2]This line alludes to Charles I, executed on January 30, 1649.

Next would I court my Liberty,
And then my birthright, Property;
But can that be, when it is known
There's nothing you can call your own?

A Reformation I would have,
As for our griefs a sov'reign salve;
That is, a cleansing of each wheel
Of state, that yet some rust doth feel;

But not a Reformation so
As to reform were to o'erthrow;
Like watches by unskilful men
Disjointed, and set ill again.

The Public Faith I would adore,
But she is bankrupt of her store;
Nor how to trust her can I see,
For she that cozens all, must me.

Since then none of these can be
Fit objects for my love and me,
What then remains but th' only spring
Of all our loves and joys, the King?

He who, being the whole ball
Of day on earth, lends it to all;
When seeking to eclipse his right,
Blinded, we stand in our own light.

And now an universal mist
Of error is spread o'er each breast,
With such a fury edg'd as is
Not found in th' inwards of th' Abyss.

Oh, from thy glorious starry wain,
Dispense on me one sacred beam,
To light me where I soon may see
How to serve you, and you trust me.

Lucasta's Fan

With a Looking-Glass in It

Estrich, thou feather'd fool and easy prey,[1]
   That larger sails to thy broad vessel need'st;
Snakes through thy guttur-neck hiss all the day,
   Then on thy iron mess at supper feed'st.

Oh what a glorious transmigration
   From this to so divine an edifice
Hast thou straight made! near from a winged stone
   Transform'd into a bird of paradise.

Now do thy plumes for hue and lustre vie
   With th' arch of heav'n that triumphs o'er past wet,
And in a rich enamell'd pinion lie,
   With sapphires, amethysts and opals set.

Sometime they wing her side, then strive to drown
   The day's eye's piercing beams, whose am'rous heat
Solicits still, till, with this shield of down,
   From her brave face his glowing fires are beat.

But whilst a plumy curtain she doth draw,
   A crystal mirror sparkles in thy breast,
In which her fresh aspect whenas she saw,
   And then her foe retired to the west,

"Dear engine that o' th' sun got'st me the day,
   Spite of his hot assaults mad'st him retreat,
No wind," said she, "dare with thee henceforth play
   But mine own breath to cool the tyrant's heat.

"My lively shade thou ever shalt retain
   In thy enclosed feather-framed glass,
And, but unto ourselves, to all remain
   Invisible, thou feature of this face!"

So said, her sad swain overheard, and cried,
   "Ye gods! for faith unstain'd this a reward!
Feathers and glass t' outweigh my virtue tried!
   Ah, show their empty strength!" The gods accord.

---

[1]*Estrich*: ostrich.

Now fall'n the brittle favourite lies, and burst.
   Amaz'd Lucasta weeps, repents, and flies
To her Alexis, vows herself accurs'd
   If hence she dress herself but in his eyes.

To Lucasta

Ode Lyric

Ah, Lucasta, why so bright,
Spread with early streaked light!
If still veiled from our sight,
What is 't but eternal night?

Ah, Lucasta, why so chaste!
With that vigour, ripeness grac'd!
Not to be by man embrac'd
Makes that royal coin embas'd,[1]
And this golden orchard waste.

Ah, Lucasta, why so great!
That thy crammed coffers sweat;
Yet not owner of a seat
May shelter you from Nature's heat,
And your earthly joys complete.

Ah, Lucasta, why so good,
Bless'd with an unstained flood
Flowing both through soul and blood
If it be not understood,
'Tis a diamond in mud.

Lucasta, stay! why dost thou fly?
Thou art not bright, but to the eye,
Nor chaste, but in the marriage-tie,
Nor great, but in this treasury,
Nor good, but in that sanctity.

Harder than the orient stone,
Like an apparition,
Or as a pale shadow gone,
Dumb and deaf she hence is flown.

---

[1]*embas'd*: debased.

Then receive this equal doom:
Virgins strow no tear or bloom,
No one dig the Parian womb;[1]
Raise her marble heart i' th' room,
And 'tis both her corse and tomb.

To My Worthy Friend Master Peter Lely

*on That Excellent Picture of His Majesty and the Duke of York,
Drawn by Him at Hampton Court*[2]

See what a clouded majesty, and eyes
Whose glory through their mist doth brighter rise!
See what an humble bravery doth shine,
And grief triumphant breaking through each line!
How it commands the face! So sweet a scorn
Never did happy misery adorn!
So sacred a contempt that others show
To this (o' th' height of all the wheel) below,
That mightiest monarchs by this shaded book
May copy out their proudest, richest look.

   Whilst the true eaglet this quick lustre spies,
And by his sun's enlightens his own eyes;
He cares his cares, his burthen feels, then straight
Joys that so lightly he can bear such weight;
Whilst either either's passiön doth borrow,
And both do grieve the same victorious sorrow.

   These, my best Lely, with so bold a spirit
And soft a grace, as if thou didst inherit
For that time all their greatness, and didst draw
With those brave eyes your royal sitters saw.

   Not as of old, when a rough hand did speak
A strong aspect, and a fair face a weak;
When only a black beard cried villain, and
By hieroglyphics we could understand;
When crystal typified in a white spot,

---

[1]*Parian womb*: the famed white marble mines on the Greek island of Paros.
[2]*Sir Peter Lely*: (1618–1680) portrait painter whose subjects included not only
   Charles I, but also Oliver Cromwell, Charles II and assorted lords and ladies of
   the latter's court.

And the bright ruby was but one red blot;
Thou dost the things orientally the same,
Not only paint'st its colour, but its flame:
Thou sorrow canst design without a tear,
And with the man his very hope or fear;
So that th' amazed world shall henceforth find
None but my Lely ever drew a mind.

Elinda's Glove

Sonnet

Thou snowy farm with thy five tenements!
    Tell thy white mistress here was one
    That call'd to pay his daily rents;
But she a-gathering flow'rs and hearts is gone,
And thou left void to rude possession.

But grieve not, pretty ermine cabinet,
    Thy alabaster lady will come home;
    If not, what tenant can there fit
The slender turnings of thy narrow room,
But must ejected be by his own doom?

Then give me leave to leave my rent with thee:
    Five kisses, one unto a place;
    For though the lute's too high for me,
Yet servants knowing minikin[1] nor bass
Are still allow'd to fiddle with the case.

The Lady A. L.[2]

My Asylum in a Great Extremity

With that delight the royal captive's brought
Before the throne, to breathe his farewell thought,
To tell his last tale, and so end with it,
Which gladly he esteems a benefit;
When the brave victor, at his great soul dumb,

---

[1]*minikin*: treble (in music).
[2]*A. L.*: probably Anne Lovelace, a cousin.

Finds something there fate cannot overcome,
Calls the chain'd prince, and by his glory led,
First reaches him his crown, and then his head;
Who ne'er till now thinks himself slave and poor;
For, though naught else, he had himself before;
He weeps at this fair chance, nor will allow
But that the diadem doth brand his brow,
And underrates himself below mankind,
Who first had lost his body, now his mind —

With such a joy came I to hear my doom,
And haste the preparation of my tomb,
When, like good angels who have heav'nly charge
To steer and guide man's sudden-giddy barge,
She snatch'd me from the rock I was upon,
And landed me at life's pavilion:
Where I, thus wound out of th' immense abyss,
Was straight set on a pinnacle of bliss.

Let me leap in again! and by that fall
Bring me to my first woe, so cancel all.
Ah, 's this a quitting of the debt you owe,
To crush her and her goodness at one blow?
Defend me from so foul impiety
Would make fiends grieve and furies weep to see.

Now ye sage spirits which infuse in men
That are oblig'd, twice to oblige agen,
Inform my tongue in labour what to say,
And in what coin or language to repay.
But you are silent as the ev'ning's air,
When winds unto their hollow grots repair:
Oh then accept the all that left me is,
Devout oblations of a sacred wish!

When she walks forth, ye perfum'd wings o' th' East,
Fan her, till with the sun she hastes to th' West,
And when her heav'nly course calls up the day,
And breaks as bright, descend some glistering ray
To circle her and her as-glistering hair,
That all may say a living saint shines there.
Slow Time, with woollen feet make thy soft pace,
And leave no tracks i' th' snow of her pure face.
But when this virtue must needs fall, to rise
The brightest constellation in the skies,
When we in characters of fire shall read

How clear she was alive, how spotless dead,
All you that are akin to piety
(For only you can her close mourners be),
Draw near, and make of hallow'd tears a dearth;
Goodness and Justice both are fled the earth.

If this be to be thankful, I've a heart
Broken with vows, eaten with grateful smart,
And beside this, the vile world nothing hath
Worth anything but her provoked wrath:
So then, who thinks to satisfy in time,
Must give a satisfaction for that crime;
Since she alone knows the gift's value, she
Can only to herself requital be,
And worthily to th' life paint her own story
In its true colours and full native glory;
Which when perhaps she shall be heard to tell,
Buffoons and thieves, ceasing to do ill,
Shall blush into a virgin-innocence,
And then woo others from the same offence;
The robber and the murderer, in spite
Of his red spots, shall startle into white;
All good (rewards laid by) shall still increase
For love of her, and villainy decease;
Naught be ignote,[1] not so much out of fear
Of being punish'd, as offending her.

So that, whenas my future daring bays
Shall bow itself in laurels to her praise,
To crown her conqu'ring goodness, and proclaim
The due renown and glories of her name;
My wit shall be so wretched and so poor,
That, 'stead of praising, I shall scandal her,
And leave, when with my purest art I've done,
Scarce the design of what she is begun;
Yet men shall send me home admir'd, exact,
Proud that I could from her so well detract.

Where then, thou bold instinct, shall I begin
My endless task? To thank her were a sin
Great as not speak, and not to speak a blame

---

[1]*Naught be ignote*: evil be unknown.

Beyond what's worst, such as doth want a name;
So thou my all, poor gratitude, ev'n thou
In this wilt an unthankful office do.
Or will I fling all at her feet I have,
My life, my love, my very soul a slave?
Tie my free spirit only unto her,
And yield up my affection prisoner?
Fond thought, in this thou teachest me to give
What first was hers, since by her breath I live;
And hast but show'd me how I may resign
Possession of those things are none of mine.

To Althea, from Prison

Song

When Love with unconfined wings
   Hovers within my gates,
And my divine Althea brings
   To whisper at the grates;
When I lie tangled in her hair,
   And fetter'd to her eye,
The gods, that wanton in the air,
   Know no such liberty.

When flowing cups run swiftly round
   With no allaying Thames,
Our careless heads with roses bound,
   Our hearts with loyal flames;
When thirsty grief in wine we steep,
   When healths and draughts go free,
Fishes, that tipple in the deep,
   Know no such liberty.

When, like committed linnets, I
   With shriller throat shall sing
The sweetness, mercy, majesty,
   And glories of my king;
When I shall voice aloud how good
   He is, how great should be,
Enlarged winds, that curl the flood,
   Know no such liberty.

Stone walls do not a prison make,
  Nor iron bars a cage;
Minds innocent and quiet take
  That for an hermitage;
If I have freedom in my love,
  And in my soul am free,
Angels alone, that soar above,
  Enjoy such liberty.

La Bella Bona-Roba[1]

I cannot tell who loves the skeleton
Of a poor marmoset, naught but bone, bone:
Give me a nakedness with her clothes on.

Such whose white-satin upper coat of skin,
Cut upon velvet rich incarnadin,
Has yet a body (and of flesh) within.

Sure it is meant good husbandry in men,
Who do incorporate with aëry lean,
T' repair their sides, and get their rib again.

Hard hap unto that huntsman that decrees
Fat joys for all his sweat, whenas he sees,
After his 'say,[2] naught but his keeper's fees.

Then Love, I beg, when next thou tak'st thy bow,
Thy angry shafts, and dost heart-chasing go,
Pass rascal deer, strike me the largest doe.

---

[1]*Bona-Roba*: a luxuriously attired wanton; possibly, but not necessarily, a pros-
  titute.
[2]'*say*: assay

A la Bourbon[1]

Done moy plus de pitiè ou plus de cruaulté, car sans ce Je ne puis pas vivre, ne morir[2]

Divine destroyer, pity me no more,
    Or else more pity me;
Give me more love, ah quickly give me more,
    Or else more cruelty!
       For left thus as I am,
       My heart is ice and flame;
   And languishing thus I
   Can neither live nor die!

Your glories are eclips'd, and hidden in the grave
    Of this indifferency;
And, Celia, you can neither altars have,
    Nor I a deity:
      They are aspects divine
      That still or smile or shine,
   Or, like th' offended sky,
   Frown death immediately.

Song

   Strive not, vain lover, to be fine,
    Thy silk's the silkworm's, and not thine;
You lessen to a fly your mistress' thought,
To think it may be in a cobweb caught.
   What though her thin transparent lawn
    Thy heart in a strong net hath drawn:
Not all the arms the God of Fire e'er made
Can the soft bulwarks of nak'd Love invade.

   Be truly fine, then, and yourself dress
    In her fair soul's immac'late glass:
Then by reflection you may have the bliss

---

[1]*Bourbon*: a kind of rose; also probably a dedication to a member of the House of Bourbon, which ruled France (1589–1792), hence the French epigraph.

[2]"Give me more pity, or else more cruelty, for without this I can neither live nor die." (The French spelling is archaic.)

Perhaps to see what a true fineness is,
   When all your gawderies will fit
   Those only that are poor in wit:
She that a clinquant outside doth adore,
Dotes on a gilded statue, and no more.

Lucasta Laughing

Hark how she laughs aloud,
   Although the world put on its shroud,
Wept at by the fantastic crowd,
   Who cry, One drop let fall
From her might save the universal ball.
        She laughs again
      At our ridiculous pain;
   And at our merry misery
      She laughs until she cry.
        Sages, forbear
      That ill-contrived tear,
        Although your fear
Doth barricado hope from your soft ear.
That which still makes her mirth to flow
   Is our sinister-handed woe,
Which downwards on its head doth go;
   And ere that it is sown, doth grow.
        This makes her spleen contract,
        And her just pleasure feast;
      For the unjustest act
        Is still the pleasant'st jest.

Index of First Lines